Contents

─────────── *Sentence* Feature ───────────

THE PROSE POEM IN EAST-ASIA

Edited by **Steve Bradbury, Andrea Lingenfelter, Jeffrey Angles,** and **Don Mee Choi**

Editor's Notes

Theo Hummer's "Embalm," which first appeared in *Sentence 3*, has been reprinted in *Best New Poets 2006*, from Samovar Press.

"Gathering," by Peter Conners (*Sentence 2)* has been translated into Arabic and published in *Mosaica*.

Four poems from *Sentence* have been selected by Heather McHugh to appear in *Best American Poetry 2007*: "Comma of God," by Milton Kessler (#3); "See Jack," by Russell Edson (#3); "Language Police Report," by Denise Duhamel (#4); and "A Voice from the City," by Louis E. Bourgeois (#4).

"Cemetery at Montparnasse," "Event," and "July" originally appeared in Kazim Ali's *The Far Mosque*, from Alice James Books.

Sentence 6 will include a special feature on "The Prose Poem in Italy," curated, introduced, and translated by Luigi Ballerini and Gian Lombardo.

Corrections

In *Sentence 4,* we misspelled Roxane Beth Johnson's name. Also in *Sentence 4,* we misprinted the title of Laura Chester's "Free Rein." We apologize for these errors.

Sentence Feature —
THE PROSE POEM IN EAST-ASIA

Introduction by Steve Bradbury
Edited by Steve Bradbury, Andrea Lingenfelter, Jeffrey Angles,
and Don Mee Choi

Baudelaire and his followers may have been the first to have "dreamt of the miracle of a poetic prose, musical without rhyme, supple and muscular," but the prose poem has been a familiar feature on the East-Asian literary landscape for more than three-quarters of a century and has flourished in recent decades. It is a Western import to be sure, but for some awfully good reasons, not least of which is the fact that the typographical convention of lineation, upon which formal distinctions between poetry and prose, on the one hand, and prose poetry and free verse, on the other, so literally and decisively turn, was not widely adopted in any of the East-Asian cultures until the beginning of the last century. Even more influential in militating against a natural evolution of the genre was the absence of any general terms for either poetry or prose; there were only specific verse forms or groups of forms (and very diverse ones at that) and a raft of more prosaic genres, many quite poetic, that were never thought of as constituting an all-encompass-ing whole, much less one in binary opposition to an as-yet-unformulated general concept of "poetry."

It was not until the middle of the great revolutionary decade of the 1910s that prose poetry was introduced. The first prose poems were quite naturally translations—Turgenev and Tagore were all the rage—but by the end of the Twenties, which roared in East-Asia as well as in the States, avant-garde poets in China, Japan, and Korea were making notable contributions to the genre; and Taiwan, which was then still a frontier colony of the Japanese Empire, lagged but a few years behind. Wars and revolutions, both cultural and political, often blighted the ground for decades at a time, but eventually the prose poem took root and finally flourished.

If early practitioners of the prose poem tended to view the genre as "a little poem in prose," to paraphrase the French term, contemporary practitioners have embraced the more open-ended idea of a text that plays out or exploits the often arbitrary distinctions between poetic and prose genres. With so much time and terrain to cover and such a wealth of poems to choose from, our survey of the development of the prose poem is necessarily somewhat scanty, but I think we've struck a good balance between the canonical and the cutting-edge. To ensure our offering includes the best poems and translations available, we have included a few translations that previously appeared in print elsewhere. Acknowledgments can be found at the end of our feature.

The Prose Poem in Chinese

Edited and translated by Steve Bradbury and Andrea Lingenfelter

Most literary historians are wont to date the inception of the Chinese prose poem (*sanwen shi*) to the eventful year of 1915, when a handful of Turgenev's now largely forgotten prose poems were translated into modern Chinese, but the truth of the matter is Baudelaire's oxymoronic genre went largely unnoticed and barely understood for more than a decade. This is hardly surprising in light of the welter of new forms, "isms," and other modernist initiatives that vied for reader attention in those early years of the Chinese Republic, when most literary reformers were far less interested in challenging the constraints of rhyme and meter than in waging the more urgent crusade to install the modern vernacular language as the medium of poetic expression. Small wonder then that several years passed before Chinese poets attempted to write prose poems of their own. The first full-length volume of original prose poetry did not appear until 1927, when the literary reformer Lu Xun published 22 prose poems under the vaguely Whitmanic title of *Yecao*, or *Wild Grass*. Despite the excellence of many of Lu Xun's poems, one of which we have translated for this feature, good prose poems remained rather thin on the ground until the postwar decades, when free verse became the overwhelming genre of choice among Chinese-speaking poets, thereby setting the stage for the prose poem to emerge as an edgier alternative.

First and foremost of the Chinese-speaking poets to have made the prose poem his métier was Shang Qin, who quite literally stumbled on the form in 1945 under circumstances almost as surreal as his early poetry. Press-ganged on the streets of Chengdu by soldiers of Chiang Kai-shek's Nationalist army, the fifteen-year-old conscript was locked away for a week in a warehouse bursting with modernist publications, among them Lu Xun's *Wild*

Grass, which had a formative influence on the aspiring poet. Another early influence on Shang Qin's prose poetry was the surrealist parables of Max Jacob, whose work Shang Qin began reading in the 1950s after his move to Taiwan, where Chiang Kai-shek and the remnants of his Nationalist army had retreated after China "fell" to the Communists. Although critics invariably describe Shang Qin as a surrealist, it is worth noting that much of the surrealism that characterizes the poet's early work began to fall away in the 1980s, when the Nationalist government, in anticipation of the end of martial law, brought an end to its censorship of the arts.

By 1987, when martial law was finally lifted and the island knuckled down to the messy but exhilarating task of transforming itself into a liberal democracy and consumer culture, the richness and diversity of Shang Qin's achievement had brought unprecedented attention to the prose poem and inspired a new generation of poets who, eager to explore the undiscovered country of sex, politics, "the system" and its discontents, and other hitherto proscribed and/or prosaic subjects, turned to the prose poem in growing numbers. At the forefront of this vanguard was Hsia Yü. Her many innovations with the form, which include parodies of non-literary genres, block paragraphs of unpunctuated conversation and other speech discourse, and (for lack of a better word) "latticeworks" of grammatically ambivalent words and phrases, helped to liberate the prose poem from the conventional notion of "a little poem in prose" and provided a model and inspiration for the many fine poets who have followed in her footsteps, three of whom (Jiao Tong, Hung Hung, and Ye Mimi), each from a different generation, we have included in our sampling.

Meanwhile, back on the mainland, after the Communists rose to power in 1949, Mao's ruthless subordination of "literary production" to the utilitarian task of furthering the communist revolution virtually eliminated the concept of creative writing for decades. As a result, the prose poem remained a *rara avis* until the early '90s, when an aging Deng Xiaoping, weary of the thankless task of establishing a "socialist market economy," enjoined the nation to follow the former Soviet Union in embracing capitalism and, to that end, relaxed the government's stranglehold on writers. At this point, a handful of poetic upstarts, mostly men, engineered what was tantamount to a Risorgimento of interest in the prose poem. In contrast to their counterparts in Taiwan, the PRC poets had little interest in exploring the liminal ground between prose poetry and free verse, whose distinctions were increasingly blurry. They looked to the prose poem to exploit its capacity to take on the narrative and discursive functions of full-fledged prose in the hope of thereby lending their poetry some of the currency and consequence enjoyed by fiction, the memoir, and other popular prose genres. Consequently, most of their prose poems are relatively long and, more often than not, part of a "multi-chapter" sequence, which makes it all but impossible to represent their work in a brief sampling. Nonetheless, we believe the three contemporary PRC prose poems we have translated for this feature (two by Xi Chuan, and one by He Chuanfu) will give some inkling of the quality and character of the prose poetry being written in China today.

Lu Xun (1881-1936)

The Dog's Retort

I dreamt I was walking down a narrow lane, dressed in rags, the very image of a beggar.

And a dog came yapping at my heels.

I turned my haughty head and spat,

"Shut your trap you uppity cur!"

"Oh, ho!" he laughed. "How presumptuous of me! One such as myself could never aspire to the level of man!"

"What did you say?!" I exploded, suspecting him of some outrageous insult.

"Ashamed am I, indeed, that I cannot tell tin from silver, cotton from silk, high officials from ordinary men, masters from slaves; why I don't even know..."

But I had high-tailed it out of there.

"Hey, come back here!" he shouted out after me. "We still have a lot to talk about."

I kept on running, as fast as I could, straight out of my dream, until I found myself lying again in my own bed.

[April 23, 1925]

translated by Andrea Lingenfelter

Shang Qin (China, 1930-)

Jupiter

Near the stove by the window over there, on the far side of the tumbling earth, the sky is the eye of a forlorn mother. The clouds have become inflamed. A garden hoe breaks into dance with the sound of a startled bird bolting from a hot skillet. Likewise, a child experiences a growth spurt. And the creature that just awoke from the dream of an afternoon and is now whirling in circles in the fruitless effort to bite its own tail is both a yellow dog and the planet Jupiter.

[1961]

translated by Steve Bradbury

Dog

Every time I peer out through the louvered window my eye is caught by the lane—you can hardly call it a street—that runs along the river, and I wind up staring out until evening falls and the street lamp I never seem to notice coming on grows bright, and the man with the gray dog appears in its circle of light.

Odd how I never see the dog until the man has almost reached the street lamp, when it suddenly appears at his heels and scurries to overtake him, which it does just as the man is passing the light but then it disappears—no doubt to lift a leg against the lamppost—then reappears again, only this time in front, then races on ahead faster and faster until it disappears from the circle of light.

The man who owns such a trusty and interesting dog is indeed to be envied.

Things go on like this for quite some time until one day, overcome by an irrepressible urge to say hello to the man, I venture from my little wooden hut and walk over to the street lamp to wait for him. But no sooner have I approached the lamp than I discover that I too have a trusty dog at my heels, which scurries to overtake me just as I pass the lamppost, then races on ahead faster and faster until at last it disappears in the darkness.

[1976]

translated by Steve Bradbury

The Speed of Sound

An elegy for Wang Yingxian, "drowned" in police custody, May 7, 1982

Someone leapt from a bridge.

As he was falling through the air, his body as stiff and disjointed as a prop dummy in a B movie, he suddenly stopped, a full half-second, before resuming his long free fall. The truth is that the force of his scream rebounding off the surface of the water had momentarily arrested his momentum. Which also goes a long way toward explaining why he made such a pitiful splash.

[1987]

translated by Steve Bradbury

Liu Kexiang (Taiwan, 1957-)

Tropical Rain Forest

Took a tour to a small island between the Equator and the Tropic of Cancer. Wet, humid green, ceaselessly fattening in the air. For five days running, we pass through the rain forest. There is no snow or prairie, nor hibernation, even in dreams. An ornithologist in our group is here to look for a horned osprey particular to this place, a species on the brink of extinction. Every evening as dusk descends, we call out in imitation of this bird, but all we hear is our own weak voices, sent out unanswered. Our aboriginal guide says: If there is no sound, the forest will disappear. And once again I'm too upset to sleep; I lie awake until morning when I press my cheek to Earth, spread wide my arms and hold it close.

[October 25, 1986]

translated by Andrea Lingenfelter

Hsia Yü (Taiwan, 1956-)

Rub: Ineffable

puss   today   I   heard
you calling me   returning   me   to   our   baroque
            and   promiscuous
understanding   puss   the problem
is just this   that   my   forgetfulness is   so much
like   a specter   my
sins   the very image of   an opera   my sleep   less
ness   sallies   to a wilderness
afar   the problem   puss   is this
that   if   all   my   gyrations
are   so   very   senseless
then   my softness   is
that   very   pity   my
warmth   in fact   that   very
distance   puss
my   luster   and my   skittish buffeting
are nothing   other than
your   favorite   fish

[1995]

translated by Steve Bradbury

Taking Her a Basket of Fruit

so today I go to this place and some guy there tells me not to come any more/ I tell him I didn't feel like going there anyway/ maybe other people do but hey that's their problem/ so I go back to this flat I'm renting and steam a fish/ when a friend drops by and we eat the fish/ and when we finish it he says he hasn't been feeling too good/ lost his job/ missed his train down south to find another/ these jobs just eat you alive he says/ you wind up getting a mortgage on a house buying a car and find yourself a good woman/ make some kids and when they look just like you you're afraid to show your face/ and when they don't look like you at all you feel just as embarrassed/ so then we talk for awhile about the difference between being a landlord and a tenant/ then we do it/ and he asks how many lovers do you have and am I any different/ what a stupid question I say of course you're different/ so how am I different he says/ I don't know I say you're just different that's all and if you really want to know maybe you're not so different after all/ you can tell that just by looking at me he says/ you're always waiting for the worst to happen I say/ but then when it does at least I can settle down he says/ so then we watch The Little Mermaid on the VCR/ and when she loses her voice he starts to cry/ we keep rewinding to the parts we like/ steam another fish/ and then I get out the Tarot to check his job prospects and see if we've any future together/ well you can forget about that job I say/ I know he says/ no point in even looking/ so what do I do/ there's nothing you can do but at least you can settle down now that you know the worst/ so do the cards say we'll get married or something he says/ no way I say/ the cards must be off or something besides he says how do you know what the cards are saying is really true/ look if you don't know what I'm trying to say there's no point in my saying it/ so why do you believe in them anyway/ I believe in them I say because the instant before I turn the cards over I know all the karma since the universe began is secretly being calculated down to the last decimal point/ enough of this universe stuff he says/ if it weren't for this universe stuff we wouldn't be lying here reading the cards/ I'm kind of fed up by then so I say I'm thinking of moving anyway/ well why don't you ask the cards if you'll find a place/ so I flip a card/ I will it says/ well then ask them if I can move in with you he says/ the cards say no way I say/ so then we do it again/ we don't know what else to do/ and then he leaves/ and I ain't seen him since/ maybe some day it'll play out differently but for now I couldn't say/ so then this other friend calls me up and says you know I really don't know if he loves me or not/ he loves you I say/ how do you know she says/ because he doesn't love me I say/ so then she hangs up/ and I lay the cards out again/ knowing she'll call me back before too long and say well do you love him/ sure enough she does/ and so I say I love him just to make her jealous/ knowing she'll call him up as soon as she hangs up on me and say if she loves you how come you don't love her/ and then she'll wait for him to say but I DO love her/ she's always waiting for the worst to happen too/ but at least she can settle down/ now that she knows nobody loves her/ she's kind of fed up with it all/ and so are we/ so later I move/ and I never do take her a basket of fruit

[1999]

translated by Steve Bradbury

Xi Chuan (1963-)

Misfortune

A 00000

An alley for two, he never turns his head around, but he knows anyway that
I am walking behind him.

He's ranting, reciting from memory: "Rein yourself in before you go over
the edge, your body is too frail to bear the weight of all that
anger."

He turns around, and instantly sees the purple vapor rising from the top
of my head. He shakes his head as the sun moves swiftly behind a
tree.

He says he saw a ghostly shadow behind me. (He's the kind of man who can
see the smile of an almond, or hear the song of the azaleas.)

"In August, beware of crows. In September, rise early every day." He
predicts that I will have a bright future, even though today I suffer
the petty denunciations of small-minded people.

A third person appears in the alley, and the stranger before me vanishes into
thin air. My heart skips a beat and I can't help feeling the person
walking towards me is my fate.

My fate and I brush past each other; but he will eventually overtake me in
this crumbling maze.

A crow grazes my August forehead.

I close my eyes, but I can still hear it saying: "Fear not, you are not just
yourself; myriad lives are using your body.

T 18060

Hidden drops of water. Hidden lips. Hidden castles in the air. Hidden
Mondays.

After Homer, after Milton, he longs to see all of this with blinded eyes, he longs to descend the stairs on feeble legs.

The sound of tearing paper behind his back, he turns his face. The sound of scratched glass behind his back, he distinctly calls out someone's name.

It is autumn. His friends took their era with them when they left, and autumn winds mass against his solitary figure.

Yet his dreamscape is expanding: the heavens are filled with the spirits of fallen heroes who have left nothing for the living but scraps of biography. Whoever he dreams of will live again.

Sympathy shows him another kind of reality: flames and grief, the rosy tinted dawn and the eternal Dao. He joins the ranks of History, which implies a rejection of the landscape at hand;

Which implies a rejection of the darkness before his eyes and of the violent splintering of a door in the dark. In a world of the blind, he has been *permitted* a glimpse of another reality.

He stumbles over a bucket, bumps into a wall, and with every step risks plunging into the abyss, but long ago he made himself into an abyss of his own, one containing a milk-white footpath and a banquet hall ablaze with lights.

This earth that bears him up, this earth that has borne up his ancestors and those near and dear to him, this earth needs his birth just as much as it needs his death. He has but a brief span of time to become himself.

The sound of medicine brewing on the stove reminds him of human frailty. A blind man's smile that only a blind man can see clearly.

[1997]

translated by Andrea Lingenfelter

Jiao Tong (Taiwan, 1956-)

English Subject Test Questions *from* "The National College Entrance Exam Series"

Listening Comprehension (transcribe the following; 1 point per question)

1 GIORGIO ARMANI

2 JEAN-PAUL GAULTIER

3 GUCCI

4 HERMÈS

5 DONNA KARAN

6 YVES SAINT LAURENT

7 MOSCHINO

8 EMANUEL UNGARO

9 GIANNI VERSACE

10 LOUIS VUITTON

True or False (1 point per question)

( ) 1 The chariest maid is prodigal enough if she unmask her beauty to the moon.

( ) 2 When the blood burns how prodigal the soul lends the tongue vows. These blazes, giving more heat than light, extinct in both even in their promise as it is a-making.

( ) 3 The power of beauty will sooner transform honesty from what it is to a bawd than the force of honesty can translate beauty into his likeness.

( ) 4 If a beauty wilt needs marry, marry a fool, for wise men know well enough what monsters she make of them.

( ) 5 God hath given me one face, and I make myself another.

[2000]

translated by Steve Bradbury

Hung Hung (1964-)

The Terrorist

Nearly everyone in the audience had come in and sat down when suddenly I realized I had to pee really I did and I was apologizing as I squeezed past all the people in their seats and then made a frantic dash to the men's room off the lobby and I was pissing away thinking the play had probably already started when my sixth grade teacher walked in the door and says aren't you done yet and I was still pissing away when my old platoon leader came in the door and walked over and asked me aren't you done yet and I hemmed and I hawed he left and a little more time passed and this time it was my son and he says dad I bet you're in somebody else's dream and he needs to pee but he can't cause he's asleep and you're not gonna be able to get out of here until he solves this problem and I say well that's great but how are we gonna let him in on the secret and my son cocks his head and looks real thoughtful says what if you kill me or I kill you that'll wake him up but does it have to be that extreme I asked I was feeling pretty discouraged and he says well there is one other option and he turned and left and during intermission I heard people out in the main hall talking about how some kid had hijacked an airplane and crashed it into the White House and I started crying and then they were all rushing back to their seats or taking off because the play wasn't holding their interest and there I was left standing in the men's room still pissing away I kid you not and wondering is this guy ever gonna wake up or what?

[2002]

translated by Andrea Lingenfelter

Ye Mimi (Taiwan, 1980-)

And All the Sweat is Left There

your curry is on someone else's plate　　name inscribed in someone
　　else's story
when you awake　　they will have long grown accustomed to the dark
　　humming some syrupy pop song
someone washing their hands in the bathroom next door　　squeezes their
　　soap into a fish
the persimmon he bit from　　is more golden than lion
when the weather gets this cold　　they agree to meet in sun-twist
　　fields
she says Happy New Year
but he is bored　　and has to have a smoke
a ghost nods off beneath the blackboard tree　　in punishment the
　　kittens are forced to crouch in tummies
we are mortified　　at vomiting a layer of sea
the skin of which could not be whiter
things are not like it imagined they would be　　nor are they like the
　　other way it imagined them
she wants the wind　　so he dispenses wind
he wants the fire　　so fire she dispenses
the girls hook their pinkies in the crooked lane　　hatch their secret
　　plots
day after tomorrow　　it will rendezvous with its familiar in the red
　　mailbox as agreed
best to bind them up　　for recycling
if you are tired my dear　　please play me with a tremolo harmonica

---

it longs to bear a book-bag on its back   stroll naked down the avenue
later he escorts her across the bridge   and midway
        experiences a temple
crisp as a cucumber   their brows
mock moonlight   hangs suspended in the air
he rubs her eyes rubs out a storied welt   and all the sweat is
        left there

[2004]

translated by Steve Bradbury

He Chuanfu (China, ?-)

The 24-Hour Clanging Abyss

Rain, coming down all day. You can't go anywhere.

The soul is like a grey pigeon inlaid in some iceberg, pure but bloodless.

Some of the things that were on my mind really did pack up and move out,
> they were wanting to spend some time in someone else's head for
> a change.

I didn't see them off, on account of the rain.

Anyway, I was under the impression that they were wearing sneakers, and
> carrying red-checkered umbrellas.

And it's not like they even said "ciao" to me, either.

In the morning I saw a beautiful child, she was stunning.

And so a thousand roses were bursting into flower in my brain and
> embracing the stars.

Some gifts are so perfect that, like pepper spray, they bring tears to your
> eyes.

A cup of peppermint tea begins to long for my lips,

The strawberry-vanilla cake is longing for the ants that moved away today,

My cavities long for the loquat cough syrup my granny used to brew.

I've wracked my brain for many long hours but I still can't recall the past.

There won't be a sunset tonight, on account of the rain.

And then again, maybe there will be. It has to set even though you can never
> bring it back.

An obstinate fly crawls on the window, watching the rain alone, weeping
> alone.

Has my solitude seized this moment to move into its body?

Your green eyes

Are a beetle poised on the margin of my memory.

My heart

Is a drifting dandelion seed come by chance to ornament your hair.

Hands, shoulders, lies, right and wrong in ruins.

Is that an English honeybee, or someone who doesn't know English trying
to forget me?

My headset is full of the sound of rain, the harmonica has lost its movie
ticket,

My private sky has been rotting away for 16 days now, while the public sea
glitters with transient lights.

Summer is always such an effort to get through. The guitar and the flannel
bear fall into a tearful embrace.

Care for a scotch on the rocks?

It's too late to show you my little forest of secrets.

You've lost your freedom.

In spite of itself, your ring finger flashes giddily.

Is that the rabbit come to repay a favor?

Illusions, illusions, the prairie wind is soaked to overflowing.

Isn't it true that every long road ends with a sky full of stars?

Drink some water, smile, go to bed alone, time scatters like dust in the
stopped-up pit of your stomach.

Not sad, I can still go watch the sunset, because I used to live there.

This country has no streetcars.

I'm just the kid in front of your vending machine who will never find his
change.

And you're the ice-cold can of cola in my convenience store that I'll never
have the heart to open.

[2006]

translated by Andrea Lingenfelter

The Prose Poem in Korea

Edited and translated by Don Mee Choi

Chu Yo-han's "Fireworks" (*Pullori*), published in 1919, is generally considered to be Korea's first prose poem (*sanmunsi*). This designation is somewhat problematic in that the poem was frequently described by critics of the time (and for many years after) as free verse, a confusion that is fairly understandable in light of the novelty of these prosaic imports from the West, which had far more in common with each other than either had with any of the traditional verse forms of Korea. Like Japan, Korea had two poetic traditions: one derived from the millennium-old verse forms of China and written in the classical language; the other patterned after traditional Korean songs and ballads. Chu's model for "Fireworks" was most likely Korean versions of the prose poems of Baudelaire published the year before by the poet and translator Kim Ŏk (1896-?), who played a major role in introducing French symbolist poetry and theory, which in turn had a huge influence on the poetry of the early modern Korean poets who took up the form. A good case in point is the prose poem Kim himself wrote as a prologue to his *Songs of the Medusa* (*Haep'ari ŭi norae*), a 1923 collection that is generally considered to be Korea's first book of modern poetry by a single author:

> When life's pleasure of early April arrives and seduces all my friends, it also reaches my body that is all but boneless, a mere lump of flesh, and I begin to float in the endless open sea. But my body that is not free merely rises and sinks endlessly with the tide of the wave and the wind. When I want to sing with my friends about my besieged heart, my joy and despair, my body without words, without rhyme—I can

only twist it in sorrow, rising and sinking. This is my song.
Hence, my song is sad yet beautiful.

In retrospect, Kim's "prologue" is unfashionably sentimental and overly-laden with exaggerated sighs of sorrow and languid despair, so much so that it would be all-too-easy to write this prose poem off as a late-flowering offshoot of the fin de siècle. To do so, however, would be to ignore the context in which it was written and understood by Korean readers of the time. Since 1910, Japan had ruled the peninsular country with an imperious hand and brooked no overt expressions of resistance, even from poets, who quite naturally turned to other, more oblique methods of voicing their frustration at being subject to an oppressive colonial regime. Although it is tempting to read Kim's "prologue" as an allegory of political resistance, I am not sure "resistance" is quite the right word; desperation would probably be closer to the truth. In any case, the air of despair and futility that dominates Kim's prose poem is fairly typical of early modern Korean prose poetry through much of the Japanese occupation.

The American liberation of Korea from 35 years of Japanese colonial rule did not give rise to the establishment of a democratic civil society. On the contrary, the dynamics of neo-colonization and the politics of America's "Cold War" with China and the Soviet Union embroiled the nation in a devastating civil war that left over two million Koreans dead and the country partitioned into two. Whether the prose poem survived in the communist-ruled North is anyone's guess. In South Korea, it was not until the late 1970s, when Korean frustration with the brutal dictatorships of President Park Chung Hee (1961-79) and President Chun Doo Hwan (1980-87) culminated in the pro-democracy uprising of May 1980, that Korean poets once again turned to the prose poem in force. This time, however, it was women poets who took the lead.

Central to these poets' interest in the prose poem was a mutual desire to distance their work from the traditional conventions of women's writing. I should point out that throughout Korean history poetry had been regarded as a male prerogative. Women may have written poems prior to the modern era, but the only women who could present their poetry, as part of their work, in public were female entertainers (*kisaeng*). From the early 1900s women publicly participated in literary production, but the poetry world dominated by men imposed restrictions in terms of style and content. Women poets were expected to write "female poetry" (*yŏryusi*), which depicted women's passivity, written in a gentle and refined language. As such free verse had been the normative form for women's poetry since the 1930s, the turn to the prose poem by the women writers who took up the form in the late 1970s and early 1980s not only underscored and exemplified their break with the past but gave them the innovative means of speaking out on subjects of oppression.

Perhaps the most influential of the women poets to have taken up the prose poem at this time was a university student named Ch'oe Sŭng-ja, who was first woman to publish her work in the influential journals of dissent that emerged in the late 1970s. Although Ch'oe was harshly attacked by the literary establishment, her boldly confessional poems, which were critical of the regime and touched on all manner of political and social themes and topics, helped shatter the fetters that had hitherto silenced the women poets of Korea. Less prominent but no less influential in breaking with the past was the poet Yi Yŏn-ju. Her experience as a nurse in some of the most economically and socially marginalized communities in South Korea gave her a strong social consciousness that runs throughout her poetry. Interestingly, among the communities in which she worked and wrote about

---

was Ŭijŏngbu, where devastating conditions of poverty and social alienation force many women into prostitution nearby a U.S. military base. Tragically, Yi committed suicide in 1992, which was only a year after her literary debut. The third and greatest of the Korean women poets to have distinguished themselves in the prose poem is the prominent poet and feminist critic Kim Hyesoon. Like Ch'oe Sŭng-ja, Kim began publishing her work in the journals of dissent that emerged prior to the pro-democracy uprising of May, 1980, but her prose poetry has continued to evolve ever since and is constantly breaking new boundaries in terms of both form and content. For this reason, I have included a relatively large sampling of her work.

Ch'oe Sŭng-ja (1952-)

Our Love of 197x

—No one has been able to salve the burn of that hour

Several years ago, only dust blew over the streets of Chekidong and we were not ourselves. We were always asleep or drunk or following a filthy tide, forever drifting away like a torn shoe fallen into a ditch . . . . The older male students would marry just any woman when they returned to school after finishing compulsory military service, and the fourth-year female students would get engaged to just any man, and the good young people faded away, giving off just the right kind of scent.

That late fall and early winter, the blood of longing flowed in our decrepit veins. The mother of longing was a dried up river. Fire and wine called to us. An evening whistle rippled across like the cry of a sperm whale as we roamed the empty streets of Chekidong like dogs. We rolled our eyes endlessly and marched forward even in our dreams. At times, real dogs barked like machine guns from each alley. However, in 197x, reality remained steadfast even though the mobs in our dreams carried out an armed assault. Because our bullets were made only of despair . . . .

Somehow when the school break came, when sleep came, when the deep snow came, the streets of Chekidong grew muddy, saying "Sorry, I love you." We even talked in our sleep and every time we cried, "I love you, please kill me," the mother of longing raised her thin arms and spoke softly, "Son of the world, my hand is empty. I have nothing to give you." Then we lay flat, dying, drooling silently like real dogs.

[1984]

translated by Don Mee Choi

Happy Diary

Today I'm happy. Mother got a bill of good health and I finally received payment for a translation and was introduced to a modest looking man at an afternoon gathering.

Today on Yŏŭi Island's riverside, wings got sold like inflated balloons and in the night sky of Dokokdong's Forsythia Apartment, Moon sits Stars around and serves each a glass of beer and yellow tulips giggle on the vast plain of a sleeping Giraffe with a Bong Bong cracker still in its mouth and in the Giraffe's mom's dream, her very own Pony car drives smoothly without gasoline and in the armpit of Giraffe's dad a one centimeter wing sprouts secretly…

Uncle Star, Suyŏng's uncle, I thank you thank you for today. Because you uncles have loved our nephews so much, we were able to dream and play out a scandal under Korea's everlasting blue sky.

Assarabia
Toroamitabul

[1984]

translated by Don Mee Choi

Editor's Note: Assarabia Toroamitabul is a Buddhist mantra.

Yi Yŏn-ju (1953-1992)

Dream of a Shallow Unconscious

Mother, please hide me, I'm afraid, that, sound of footsteps, maybe they are, herding, a pack of dogs, to here, Mother, go where? Mother, help me, just yesterday, just a month ago, a young man in the neighborhood, the man on the second floor, disappeared, they haven't, returned, they, uhh uhh, Mother, my, face, eyes, reflected in the window, are terrifying, my hand, is moving, unexpectedly, bit by bit, ahh, even though, I'm, not moving, the hand, is moving, it's unlocking, the door, the pack of dogs, ahh, a troop of footsteps, are coming, they'll, rape, they'll, crush, let's run away, some-where, far, Mother, where did you go, without me knowing? I should, with them, ahh, I don't want to, what did you say? that it is a sin to be alive? that we can't run away? then, I'll, ahh uhh!

[1991]

translated by Don Mee Choi

Nursery Notes

Just born and already neglected, it lies in a coffin-like cradle. Smells fishy like a butcher's shop. Who will be able to guide the infants to a faraway place, through the many trials of life until they reach the silence of the aged? I fill up the washbasin and wash my hands.

When the lights are off, this place remains in darkness. Even the infant born yesterday was pulled from the uterus like a potato; they're all alike. Or the whole body is anesthetized for a cesarean and the time of birth is announced, the hour when an infant is sent out onto a battlefield like a foot soldier. I pick up an infant and watch the spots on its face fill with yellow pus.

Shielding your body with guns and knives is not hard, the problem is finding the strength to resist naked without praying. But then prayers are only written for the dead . . . . I rub my hands briskly with a cotton ball soaked in alcohol. Please don't forget how thoroughly the light hides the immense darkness . . . .

[1991]

translated by Don Mee Choi

When in Need of a Chisel and a Hammer

One man sat, stooped over. His shoulders quivered in silence. Another man cried. Two men stood in a dark alley. In a suicide game, they struck each other with their huge fists. Stabbing each other in the side and chest, they changed positions. Mannequins inside the display box staggered. And young women hid under the overcoats of young men their age. "The thunder of footsteps is terrifying. Why is it louder at night?" The young men pushed their tongues into the mouths of the young women, and they shared a hard, disturbing sensation. You need a chisel and a hammer to break a hole through the wall because it is reinforced with concrete and steel. As I was walking I thought, "But where must we go in order to turn in our lump of fattened flesh for a chisel and a hammer?" The sky fluttered as if it were starved and the stars crumbled into silver confetti . . .

[1991]

translated by Don Mee Choi

Kim Hyesoon (1955-)

The Cultural Revolution Inside My Dream

The main ingredient of my social standing is reaction
Night after night I go to school to write the confession of my crime
My lover, a photon, is a Red Guard who enjoys digging
The photon has many lovers, dispatched from the sun
to the inside of my dream, maybe it's a prison guard or a murderer
After copulation, it devours its lovers
Even though my crime grows day by day, there is always more left

I'm so exhausted today. My eyelids feel like a ton of bricks and my ears pull down the shutters, the photon that has been pacing outside my dream knocks on the door. "Photon, please, I'm very tired today." After a long day of roaming inside sunlight and being crushed by the photon as flat as a screen, the photon inserts a confessional program into my body. "I'm too sick today, just forgive me, please." The photon makes a hole in my body, goes deep into my flesh with a spade and bangs on my bones. The photon that is as bright as a star. The photon that flickers on the TV screen after the broadcast has ended. The photon calls my name, gets furious at me, encircles me, blabs to its heart's content. The confession that I write again and again. The photon enjoys itself, uses the waterfall of my blood as its mirror. I've written so many confessions that I don't know what's what. Things are mixed up to the point that my father is transformed into my child. How wonderful it would be to sleep even one night outside the house of the photon. A few decades ago, when I used to work for a publisher, I went to City Hall to get the manuscripts inspected. The Mr. Military Officers would

hand them back after smearing black ink all over them. Sometimes all but
the titles were blackened. Where did all the blackened Mr. Officers go?

The photon plays all night, using the inside
of my body as a screen, and today it has made
my dead grandmother much younger than me
Grandmother took out a charcoal briquette from the furnace
then replaced it with the full moon on fire
Inside the room, Mother lay down after giving birth and cried
There were people inside each teardrop, so I asked,
"Who are you?" They replied that they were Mother's spirits
But when I peered into the teardrops, the people were all me
Inside the closed school, I was sitting on all the benches
reading aloud from my confessions, and the voice informed me that
Grandmother grows up and becomes Mother
and Mother grows and becomes me
There are so many of me that I feel like I'm going to die
Every night the all of me as a collective
goes to school to write confessions
goes to the photon to get censored

[1985]

translated by Don Mee Choi

Seoul's Dinner

Flowers enter. The flowers with puckered lips. The flowers that fill the back of a truck suck on the wall of the tunnel. The tunnel reddens momentarily. She plucks off the new leaves and shoves them into her mouth. Angelica shoots drop from angelica trees and fall into the dish of seasoned soy sauce. A truckload of angelica enters. Angelica shoots dye the mouth of Seoul green. Flatfish enter. A thousand flatfish packed in ice enter, swooning. A truckload of the East Sea enters. Pigs enter. The pigs oink and suck on Seoul's lips. She dips the meat from the pig's neck in pickled shrimp and eats. Her squirming throat is omnivorous. Eels pour in like a muddy stream. The Taebaek range is shredded and enters, squirming. The farms of the lower ranges of Mount S lhak enter, salted. Radishes revealing only the top half of their white bottoms are neatly stacked onto a truck. Trucks with their lights on enter. They line up and enter in between the teeth. When the trucks leave the tunnel, Seoul's blue stomach acid embraces them. Some of the trucks try to make their way through the sea of acid, but the darkness inside Seoul's intestine is dense. Vegetables in sacks enter. Thousands of chickens with reddened crowns follow thousands of eggs just laid today and enter. Bulls as big as elephants their eyes fiercely opened enter. Bulls charge the path inside the body of someone who lives in Seoul. Tonight she drinks too much rice wine. The tunnel where the wine is poured is long and dark. White milk that could overflow a nursery pours out of the tunnel into the night's intestine. The plains of Honam enter. But in the opposite lane, the trucks loaded with waste water purifiers have lined up in single file. Having left the drinking party, I begin to vomit as soon as I step outside. Seoul eats and shits through the same door. My body curls up like a worm. It seems that every few days a big hand descends from the sky to roll out cloud-like toilet paper and wipe the opening of Seoul, which is simultaneously a mouth and an anus. Tonight, fat flakes fall as the last train leaves the tunnel. I let the snow collect, then shove it into my mouth.

[1995]

translated by Don Mee Choi

Face

There is another you inside you.

The you inside you pulls you tight into the inside, so your fingernails curl inward and your outer ears swirl into the inside of your body. You would probably leave this life the moment the you inside you lets go of the hand that grabs you.

Your face stays frozen in motion as the you inside you pulls you hard. At times, that face leans towards mine outside of you and I can feel the you inside you, looking at me from the inside of your eyes; but the you inside you has never once let go of the hand that grabs you. As always you are pulled tight. Now your face has deep creases from the strain.

The you inside you is so strong that the I inside me is about to get dragged into your inside.

You are now drinking a glass of wine, holding a piece of cheese in your hand.

The I inside me thinks about the fact that the cheese is made of milk then worries about which cow inside the cow has spurted out the milk.

Even if you are far away, another you inside you is here. I can't return or avoid the you inside you.

Maybe I am the hostage of an absent being.

I would certainly stay alive while the I inside me clutches onto me; furthermore, I want to offer the cheese made of me inside me on your table every morning.

[2001]

translated by Don Mee Choi

Hen

Rain hammers away at the keyboard till it's all bloody. Red mud splatters. Trees fall and the chickens tremble inside the water-filled coop. She hammers away till the keyboard is bloodied. She hammers away so hard that a crimson flower of flesh blooms on top of her skull. The crown flutters like a flag—her heart placed on top of her head. The lit window screams because the light in the room was turned off at one point. Her typewriter-teeth endlessly collect the feed onto the paper. She lowers her head, feels her forehead. Three women left home today. They left the coop crying. You all know where they have been taken to. She spreads her ten fingers and clutches her desk, types the tears one at a time. Night arrives and the rain stops momentarily. Her beloved's leather shoes drop outside the window and she lays an egg while hammering away at the keyboard. The conveyer belt swiftly takes away her egg. She mustn't go outside. Today her body, the book of pain, has barely made it through a page of flesh, bleeding. However, the calendar she pecks out each day is still on the same page. Why is she making a calendar that no one looks at? Her eyes want to sleep, so they close slowly from the bottom to the top. Outside the window, the rain, as if it had been waiting, begins to hammer away at the keyboard. Blood splatters on the window. Her eyes flash open and her heart, a loop of painful blood vessels, flinches and bleeds on top of her head. The crown turns crimson once more.

[2001]

translated by Don Mee Choi

An Old Fridge

I'm desperately holding back the urge—my feet want to reach you before me. I'm desperately holding back the urge—my lips want to reach you before me. I've held back like this for decades. It's strange when I think about it. It seems that I've been holding back since I got a fridge of my own. Anyhow, I've been thinking. My head is completely filled with ice. Anyone who touches my cold feet faints. The lips of those who enter my heart freeze. Therefore, I won't move even one step from here. I won't hold out my arms to anyone. I thought to myself that I won't forget any of this. Because I'm desperately holding back like this not a single leaf drops in my room, not a single bird can take off from the ground. I'll hold out with my fingers plugged into the 220-volt outlet even if the wind blows. The frozen painting of a landscape—how beautiful! The ice princess of the ice world inside the landscape—how pure! I won't worry even if blood drips down her thighs because it will freeze right away. It's hot outside and cold inside. It's so cold that it's boiling. When the door opens, I'm so startled that I turn on the light—frozen intestines hang from the winter landscape. The power has been out for several days because of the typhoon, and for decades I've been acting as if nothing's wrong till the inside of my body begins rotting away.

[2002]

translated by Don Mee Choi

The Prose Poem in Japan

Edited by Jeffrey Angles

Japan has had a long tradition of poetic prose that stretches back to at least the Heian period (794-1185). One of the most beloved examples, *The Pillow Book of Sei Shōnagon* (*Makura no sōshi*), a diary-like work written by a lady-in-waiting in early eleventh-century court, consists of short, poetic fragments that retain their freshness even a millennium later. Although one purpose of this book was to organize ideas for poetry and present snippets of poetry with some explanatory text, *The Pillow Book* and other later hybrids of prose and poetry such as the travel diaries (*haibun*) of Matsuo Bashō were precursors to the prose poem only in the sense that they have occasionally provided models for Western poets.

Until the late nineteenth century, Japanese poetry consisted of several distinct traditions, each with its own set of rules and norms. Japanese writers could write in *kanshi*, a type of poetry in classical Chinese governed by complicated prosodic rules first borrowed from China then modified in Japan. The Japanese also had their own indigenous poetic forms, such as *waka* (also known as *tanka* in the modern period), *renga,* and *haiku*, which were comprised of various metrical phrases of five and seven mora.[1] Traditionally, none of these forms of poetry were written with lineation; instead, they appeared as long lines of text broken only by their internal structure.

Around 1860, Japan began to open to external influences after a long period of isolation, and this led to an increased exchange in many areas, including literature. Japanese writers became excited with the possibilities the longer, freer, Western forms of poetry might offer. The result was the development of a new genre of poetry, which the Japanese called *shi*, for which the Japanese borrowed the Western concept of lineation.

Japanese poets of *shi* did not start writing prose poems right away; however, the development of entire genre of *shi* in the late nineteenth and early twentieth centuries involved breaking away from the codified meter and language of traditional poetry and slowly moving toward something that resembles the longer, freer forms of prose. By the early 1910s, poets like Kawaji Ryūkō (1888-1959) had jettisoned the classical language and traditional metrical patterns for "colloquial free verse." It was in the 1920s that Japanese writers started composing colloquial poetry in unlineated blocks of relatively prosaic text (*sanbun-shi*). Although there had been turn-of-the-century translations of Baudelaire and Rimbaud, the poet Hagiwara Sakutarō (1889-1942) is sometimes considered the first author to write modern Japanese prose poetry.

The form quickly caught on amongst modernist poets. In these early prose poems, the focus of experimentation was breaking with the metrical and diction-related conventions of the past. Scholar Dennis Keene notes that if one sets aside the typographical and graphological experimentation of dadaist and futurist poets, "the making of the prose poem seems to have been the supreme modernist act for the Japanese poet... The prose poem, by definition, denies the rhythmical values which have dominated the lyrical tradition."[2]

Many of the prose poems by Sakutarō and other modernist authors such as Anzai Fuyue (1898-1965), Kitagawa Fuyuhiko (1900-1990), and Inagaki

Taruho (1900-1977) have a strong narrative component. Most seem to have conceived of the prose poem as a cinematic snippet of writing, more like a mini-story or *conte* laden with visual images and poetic resonance than a form that might experiment with syntax or semantics. These are, of course, exceptions; for example, the modernist poet Haruyama Yukio (1902-1994) created a prose poem that consisted of a single, syntactically complex sentence that runs to over twenty pages in length. Still, like in the West, the prose poem and short fiction were so closely related throughout the 1920s and 1930s that the dividing line between the two was at times virtually non-existent. For instance, the writings of Kajii Motojirō (1901-1932), which are generally considered fiction today, were labeled "prose poetry" upon their first publication. Perhaps as a result of this legacy, the Japanese prose poem tends to have an especially strong narrative quality even today. One sees this in the work of contemporary poets Kasuya Eiichi, Tada Chimako, and Hirata Toshiko translated in this feature.

In contemporary Japan, the prose poem remains an important form of literary production. In fact, virtually ever major poet of *shi*, regardless of stamp and persuasion, has tried his or her hand at prose poetry. This means that anyone interested in collecting a handful of prose poems for a collection like the one you now hold in your hands faces a dizzying array of choices. The following selection displays some of the many vibrant and original directions the prose poem has taken in contemporary Japan.

---

[1] Western writers commenting on traditional Japanese poetic forms often mistakenly describe mora as "syllables"; however the method of counting units of sound in Japanese is profoundly different from the method of counting syllables in Western languages. For instance, in Japanese poetics, the sound "n" could stand as one, independent unit of sound and a long vowel could count as two. It is therefore wrong to say (as commonly believed) that haiku in Japanese consist of a pattern of 5-7-5 syllables; one should instead say that it consists of 5-7-5 moras.

[2] Dennis Keene, Introduction, *The Modern Japanese Prose Poem* (Princeton UP, 1980), 13-14.

Kasuya Eiichi (1934-)

Summers and Bridges

Consider a single man; the death that approaches for him comes but once; however, consider a single town; the summer that approaches surely does not come just once.

Still, just as it is possible for a single town to have but a single bridge, a single man may have but one single summer.

As he welcomed the summer with hat pulled low, what was it that he most feared, that he thirsted after most? Surely, the world was aware.

And this is why. For he who had thoroughly resigned himself to the knowledge that freedom is a crime, and death a promise, here upon this bridge was the place where he thought most single-mindedly of escape.

> From there, the town was visible. The town of gloomy windows in gloomy towers.
> From there, the town was visible. The town where gloomy towers opened their gloomy windows.

Summer comes to all towns from the ships at sea, from the ears of barley in the fields.

Still, there are endings, when on a nameless bridge a single man is shot with the sound of a single bullet. Endings to single, steel summers unknown to a single other soul.

[1975]

translated by Jeffrey Angles

Takahashi Mutsuo (1937-)

From *Verbs I* and *Verbs II*

To eat

> God eats us. We eat God. We all eat each other.

To lead

> The one who leads will always have the divine profile of that beautiful young man; silently, he will lead us to things, to that twilight territory without shadows.

To point

> To point… By the act of pointing, we disdain, we cause someone to decay. When he who has been pointed out has decayed completely, then the act of pointing is complete. Another possibility is that by pointing, one who has been pointed out stops his own process of decay.

To look at one another

> I look at you. You look at me. I look at the me that is in you. You look at the you that is in me. I look at the you that is in me that is in you. You look at the me that is in you that is in me. I look at the me that is in you that is in me that is in you… You look at the you that is in me that is in you that is in me… In the end, the you and I that are looking at each other are really looking at nothing at all.

[1974 and 1978]

translated by Jeffrey Angles

Suzuki Shirōyasu (1935-)

In My Mouth

as I turn off the late night TV   I want to separate myself from my mother tongue   I wake up alone   stand up in my room   pull a foreign book off the shelf and begin to pronounce the sounds inside   as I pronounce them I sit on the toilet

I begin to feel as if it is slipping gradually from my backside into the water   my mother tongue is fading away   the sequence of pronounced sounds looks like the simplistically smooth bottom of the pool of water   it forms a fragile membrane   the vowels make me aware of the space inside my oral cavity   they continue the shape inside my mouth   the book in my hands is in a foreign tongue   meaning remains in spatters   a pillar of water erupting   upon the desk   a harbor breakwater   I turn the page the bodies of nude women turn round and round in my dreams   one of them trips inside my mouth   the sound of an "r"   suddenly   from her hair   the woman's body splits open and breaks into bloom like a lily   she has walked too far

the clouds of afternoon surge forth   the sharp beak of a bird pierces my side   what is recorded here in this book?   the crystal hewn from the earth is stuffed into bags of hemp and piled into boats   the workers in the harbor are not satisfied by the women they buy   endlessly they seek out love   I continue to pronounce   space forms inside my mouth   and stays for good

[1977]

translated by Jeffrey Angles

Itō Hiromi (1955-)

The Maltreatment of Meaning

Can you speak Japanese?

No, I cannot speak

Yes, I can speak

Yes, I can speak but cannot read

Yes, I can speak and read but cannot write

Yes, I can speak and write but cannot understand

I was a good child

You were a good child

We were good children

That is good

I was a bad child

You were a bad child

We were bad children

That is bad

To learn a language you must replace and repeat

I was an ugly child

You were an ugly child

We were ugly children

That is ugly

I am bored

You are bored

We are bored

That is boring

I am hateful

You are hateful

We are hateful

That is hatred

I will eat

You will eat

We will eat

That is a good appetite

I won't eat

You won't eat

We won't eat

That is a bad appetite

I will make meaning

You will make meaning

We will make meaning

That is conveying language

I will use Japanese

You will use Japanese

We will use Japanese

That is Japanese

I want to rip off meaning

You want to rip off meaning

We want to rip off meaning

That is the desire to rip off meaning

I want to show contempt for language as nothing more than raw material

You want to show contempt for language as nothing more than raw material

We want to show contempt for language as nothing more than raw material

That is, language is nothing more than raw material

I will replace words mechanically and make sentences impossible in real life

You will replace words mechanically and make sentences impossible in real life

We will replace words mechanically and make sentences impossible in real life

That is replacing words mechanically and making sentences impossible in real life

Rip off meaning

Sound remains

Even so we search for meaning. The primitive reflection of a newborn sucking a finger if one sticks one out

It is the primitive reflection of a newborn sucking a finger if I stick one out

It is the primitive reflection of a newborn sucking a finger if you stick one out

It is the primitive reflection of a newborn sucking a finger if we stick one
out

It is the primitive reflection of sucking if a newborn that sticks out a finger

As for me, meaning

As for you, meaning

As for us, meaning

Is meaning, that is

Do not convey

As for me, do not convey

As for you, do not convey

As for us, do not convey

Do not do it, that is conveyance

Meaning ripped apart and covered in blood is surely miserable, that is
happiness

I am happy meaning covered in blood is miserable

You are happy meaning covered in blood is miserable

We are happy meaning covered in blood is miserable

The blood-covered meaning of that is blood-covered misery, that is
happiness

[1991]

translated by Jeffrey Angles

Hirata Toshiko (1955-)

Maid

If it frightens me this much to have broken a measly plate, then it goes without saying that I wouldn't have it in me to commit murder.

This is a one-hundred-year-old plate.

No matter how much Madam cherished this plate, its time had just about come. Madam will not see it this way, however.

If she learned the plate was broken, she would probably whip me.

Madam's whip is extremely painful.

I won't be able to get up for a week.

There are some who never get up again.

Fortunately she wasn't home when it happened, so I left in a hurry, giving up on this month's salary.

I was terribly frightened.

I was so frightened, in fact, that I put on Madam's dress, put her shoes on my feet, and filled my bag with fistfuls of her jewels.

And boarded a bus headed far, far away. On the bus I continued to be frightened.

It was the Master's fault in the first place. It was he that told me to spike

---

⚙ Sentence 5

poison in Madam's drink. I had always been told by my agent that I am not to disobey the Master, and Madam is not one to be felled by poison anyway. So I simply obeyed. And then Madam disappeared. I hadn't heard of any travel plans. I hadn't helped her prepare to go out.

I was so concerned about where she had gone, that my hands slipped, and my fingers lost their grip on the plate. And then in a split second, the plate fell and shattered like fireworks. The plate was one hundred years old, so it must have been ready to break.

I wonder if Madam has returned already. If she has noticed the broken plate.

If Madam was going to remain absent, I wouldn't have had to escape the mansion in such a hurry. But any small mishap always reaches her ears. And then she would return right away, with her face flushed. With plenty of new whips.

The Master said that he would reward me. That if I obeyed his commands, he would reward me with lots of punishments. I like the Master's punishments. At first my whole body shook in fear. Now, my body shakes in joy. I obeyed his commands, but I haven't received my reward yet.

I fled from the mansion in a hurry, leaving behind the plate as well as my reward. I have a broken plate to clean. I have a reward from the Master to receive. I am a maid. The maid's job is to clean the rooms, and be rewarded. I must once again put on my white apron, sit silently jostled on the bus driven by the deaf and mute man, and smile, flutter my way back to that mansion tilting over with enormous debt.

[1997]

translated by Sawako Nakayasu

Yuko Minamikawa Adams (1966-)

from The way things were with Mr. Pophwell

Up to January 10, 2000

Mr. Pophwell
wins in an auction bid the medal of the veteran who enjoys his appreciation
of the mailbox upon which he has put a skirt, which shelters the parents of
the Chinese cabbage who failed in the sneak attack of the pliers that pull
teeth from the portrait of the piranha that has been fretworked on a maple
tree that fans the chartered bus run amok with Martians who picked the
pupils growing on a plum tree.

Up to January 24, 2001

Mr. Pophwell
is frightened by the shadow of the starling that pecks at the spirit filling the
crystal ball that senses the changes of the times in the sudden sobbing of the
exhaust fumes that live alongside the loam layer of the Kant Region that
tries to throw off the starting time of the civil service examination which
requires one to write, in under fifty characters, their first impressions of the
eyelashes of the taxi driver that shares with all his relatives a festival, direct
from the source.

[1998]

translated by Sawako Nakayasu

Abe Hinako (1953-)

Terribly-Thin Heartlessness/Inframince

—*For Marcel Duchamp*

– 1 –

numbers of lovers growing by happy chance
all probably feeding upon dizziness
with their izoid temperaments
stopping short of stepping on thin ice
lateral intercourse with all
diffuse brownian motion
names grown thin
up high in the sky
swift kisses
dazzling
companionship
scratches
thin
skin
μ

– 2 –

Taken in by sweet words, Stella comes to the summer house on the solstice festival
Wearing the latest silk dress to show off the serpentine curves of her willowy spine
In the great hall, men and women once called prodigies bustle about noisily
Stella's apparel and comportment are somewhat lacking in polish
But if you think about what social sophistication really is then you'll see that
In the end it is only adhering persistently to a certain kind of passive attitude
The use of competing allegories (being as light as possible on the nouns
Inserting plenty of adjectives and not tripping over the ends of your verbs)
What are the prodigies of yesteryear saying as they smile and dance?
News of laid-off acquaintances, collections of paper scraps, and grandiloquent bragging about work
Taking revenge while joking all the while, killing some half-baked know-it-all with kindness
All of it is idle chatter far beneath her, but Stella cannot see through it
When Stella hears insinuating remarks that the scarlet dress glued to
Her glamorous body with sweat should be the prison garb of a habitual drug-user, she is hurt
She falls, her tumble precipitated by a constellation of grotesque rumors
Her dress, ripped at the seams, like a torn moth on the threshold, swept down into the garden

– 3 –

numbers of lovers continually growing by happy chance
naked bodies descending a staircase while sleepwalking
and stepping into a picture of bathers
the rampancy of perspective makes
the headaches of the peeping tom
ever more difficult
too many bachelors
even if given
prescripts for
latent enmity
fake high spirits
the radius
of a gaze
wildly
reflects
ripples
of li-
ght

– 4 –

After rolling onto the terrace, Stella collapses into a rattan chair and looks at the garden
On such an evening, with its purple clouds tracing stripes across the western sky,
Somewhere surely a rust-colored moth is perched on a pin, fluttering its thin wings
Stella, who has descended into the lingering summer garden, turns to the summer house
In the light rectangle of the open window she sees the figures like miniature portraits stirring
With an indistinct hurt in her heart, she begins walking along the gravel path
The spacious garden slopes gradually down until it reaches the surrounding wall
On the other side of the wall stretches a flat field full of tall, pointed weeds
The choking aroma of the shrubby undergrowth, fleur-de-lis, jasmines,
Honeysuckles, irises, stocks and ferns all jumbled together enfolds her
Darkness has already descended when Stella enters the field through a hole in the wall
Her hands push aside the ocean of grass wet with dew, her feet trod upon it
Shivering in the wet air of the summer night, Stella throws herself into the brush
She presses her lips onto the black earth, shakes her hair free, and tears her dress
With no underwear underneath, her genitals are exposed to the starlight
Thighs open and head craned to the left, she takes on the distorted nocturnal pose of sleep

– 5 –

numbers of lovers continually growing by happy chance
she smiles with thin lips that try to register
but will probably fail in the attempt
expectantly waiting for caresses
whether excited or not
then she turns over and faces up
legs spread out wide
at an unnatural angle
like in the photo
her weatherbeaten
groin hairless
unripe and
c o n –
c a v e

[2001]

translated by Jeffrey Angles

Tatehata Akira (1947-)

The Dog of Zero Degree

The dog of zero degree colors our shame. One half of him is a garden's crime and the other half a gray girl's politics, I was told. That was the only reason he becomes our coloration. Miss Koike ought to have known that too. Let's proceed together, I said. Let's proceed together to find a good spectacle. There ought to be a dog much lower, a hedge much lower, a garden much lower.

As a matter of fact, on a certain day in the future, there was a low dark pond. It was so much a place for the dog of zero degree that it almost made you laugh. If someone's consciousness smiles at the garden's crime, it will be extolled as the severe spectacle of the age. A girl's politics is something like that. The soldiers for hire with long necks will also fall silent... Miss Koike, you ought to know that. Near the dark pond the dog of zero degree emerges. A quiet spectacle, an admirable spectacle, and political girls...

We got off at a gray station. That too was a certain day in the future. Utility poles were looking down upon a twisted, deserted shopping district. The low dark pond should be a little beyond of it. It couldn't be that far. The probability theory that belongs to spectacles proves that. Theoretically speaking, the crime of making someone smile... Come, let's go find a good spectacle. Let's go look for a gray girl with skinny arms.

At that distance now, the dog of zero degree is baying.

[2004]

translated by Hiroaki Sato

Selected Works in English

Bradbury, Steve. *Feelings Above Sea Level: Prose Poems from the Chinese of Shang Qin*. St. Paul, MN: Zephyr Press, 2006.

Bradbury, Steve. *Fusion Kitsch: Poems from the Chinese of Hsia Yü*. St. Paul, MN: Zephyr Press, 2001.

Choi, Don Mee, trans., *Anxiety of Words: Contemporary Poetry by Korean Women*. St. Paul, MN: Zephyr Press, 2006.

Choi, Don Mee, "Korean Women—Poetry, Identity, Place: A Conversation with Kim Hyesoon," in *positions: east asia cultures critique*. Winter 2003: 529-539.

Choi, Don Mee, trans., *When the Plug Gets Unplugged: Poems by Kim Hyesoon*. Kaneohe, HI: Tinfish Press, 2005.

Gardner, William O. *Advertising Tower: Japanese Modernism and Modernity in the 1920s*. Cambridge: Harvard University Asia Center, 2006.

Hartman, Charles. "Poetry," *The Indiana Companion to Traditional Chinese Literature*. Bloomington: Indiana UP, 1986: 53-74.

Hirata, Hosea. *The Poetry and Poetics of Nishiwaki Junzaburo: Modernism in Translation*. Princeton: Princeton UP, 1993.

Kaldis, Nicholas. "The Prose Poem as Aesthetic Cognition: Lu Xun's *Yecao*," *Journal of Modern Literature in Chinese* 3.2. January 2000: 43-82.

Keene, Dennis, ed. and trans., *The Modern Japanese Prose Poem: An Anthology of Six Poets*. Princeton: Princeton UP, 1980.

McCann, David R. *The Columbia Anthology of Modern Korean Poetry*. New York: Columbia UP, 2004.

Nienhauser, Jr., William H. "Prose," *The Indiana Companion to Traditional Chinese Literature*. Bloomington: Indiana UP, 1986: 93-120.

Sas, Miryam. *Fault Lines: Cultural Memory and Japanese Surrealism*. Palo Alto, CA: Stanford UP, 1999.

Ueda, Makoto. *Modern Japanese Poets and the Nature of Literature*. Palo Alto, CA: Stanford UP, 1983.

van Crevel, Maghiel. "Fringe Poetry, But Not Prose: Works by Xi Chuan and Yu Jian," *Journal of Modern Literature in Chinese* 3.2. January 2000: 7-42.

van Crevel, Maghiel. "Matter over Mind—On Xi Chuan's Poetry," http://www.thedrunkenboat.com/crevel.html

Yeh, Michelle. "From Surrealism to Nature Poetics: A Study of Prose Poetry from Taiwan," *Journal of Modern Literature in Chinese* 3.2. January 2000: 119-156.

Yeh, Michelle. "'Variant Keys' and 'Omni-Vision': A Study of Shang Qin," *Modern Chinese Literature* 9.2. Fall 1996: 327-67.

Acknowledgments

A few of the translations in this feature were previously published. Grateful acknowledgment is made for permission to reprint the translations of the following works:

Steve Bradbury: Shang Qin's "The Speed of Sound," from *Circumference: Poetry in Translation*, and Hsia Yü's "Rub: Ineffable" and "Taking Her a Basket of Fruit," from *Fusion Kitsch: Poems from the Chinese of Hsia Yü*. St. Paul, MN: Zephyr Press, 2001. By permission of Steve Bradbury.

Don Mee Choi: Ch'oe Sŭng-ja's "Our Love of 197x," from *Bamboo Ridge*, and Kim Hyesoon's "Seoul's Dinner," from *When the Plug Gets Unplugged* by Kim Hyesoon. Kaneohe, HI: Tinfish Press, 2005. By permission of Don Mee Choi.

Andrea Lingenfelter: Liu Kexiang's "Tropical Rain Forest," from *Frontier Taiwan: An Anthology of Modern Chinese Poetry*, edited by Michelle Yeh and N.G.D. Malmqvist. New York: Columbia UP, 2001. By permission of Andrea Lingenfelter.

Hiroaki Sato: Tatehata Akira's "The Dog of Zero Degree," from *Poetry Kanto*. By permission of Hiroaki Sato and Alan Botsford Saitoh of *Poetry Kanto*.

Mark Yakich

Patriot Acts

Whoever duct-taped kitty with the C-4 thought himself a genius. And who wouldn't want to send in an animal to do an animal's job? By a mortar lake and a budding sky, kitty stood there with birdshit on her head. Bullets brushed by and plastic bags rippled in place of flags. She swayed back and forth at the entrance of the hotel. And then, worthy of a copyeditor's pun— catastrophe! A bullet hit the kitten killing her instantly, saving many people. But what's left us now? I invite you, compatriot, to stroke this paper as you would have her corpse. Don't just toss her into the recycling bin because she didn't finish her mission.

Robert Strong

[Untitled]

George Bush is uh big dull la-zy dumb guy—trochaic pentameter waiting to attack you like a pteradactyl: accidental: knock you off the scenic overlook with a soaring pyrrhic foot. George Bush, unstressed. Sure, I'd drink lite beer with him and watch tv, like to bark harmless spondees at the pom-poms. But when the form of prodigal-son-saved takes on its rehearsed falling rhythm, I'm off. See ya, George. Poor Bush: dyslexic and married to a librarian whose resumé insists she's never been fetishized—and (George thinks) never limericked, *that's icky and sinful.* She took his last name anyway. Me, I feel this form should remain unjustified—George started it—but those in charge think undelineated theories of a democratic moment need, at least, to control their own borders. Rigidly, it's blind justified to the right. I apologize. Since the subject is really his royal assonance, be prepared for half-, for slant that's nearly spin and categorically off. Listen: any wrenched accent occurs when the requirements of metrical stress can't translate Greenwich, Connecticut to goddam Texas.

[Untitled]

Ha ha I saw you go into the voting booth, John Wilkes. The curtains closed for you this first snowy day and then there was silence. Ha ha, John, there is no applause for your democracy. No privacy is not something you can control—it picks the flavors for licking. The curtain opens on a mechanical arm sealing your own suggestions for fate on the patient roll of paper. Some paper was made to never be confetti, get it. Tomorrow, the newspapers—then essays, articles, archives, encyclopedias, and, at last a cute & tragic piece for high school theater. Ha ha, I see you up on stage, Johnny, you are such a drama queen, sexually ambiguous, bursting out of yourself, out of character, onto everyone in the audience dying for applause. You kill me.

[Untitled]

Skadoodle, Bamboozle—we saw you. The tonic you peddle did not take to us and we ain't gonna just go home. We are massing to be inciteful & aimed in the right direction with what we still call hate. It's a good thing. Hate, gay, green, left right liberal wing & jell-o pudding—we reserve words in our arsenal of original meanings. You can't tell us, mammytapper, what to tell. You're boring and paid for like sneakers from Caldors. Listen: nigger, nigga, brother, poor—we help a man out no matter what for. Shitstain your champagnepants, you cyborg. You bureaucratic blackbutthole, un-fun syntax twister, you powerfront. Dear Status-Shield, we hereby disregard your wardrobe of do's & don't's. We maintain ourselves the monkeybars. We swing here for free while you sit on your nightstick and finger the gasmask, hoping we'll slip up some letter of the law. We saw you—will sleep-at-night you—know where you live among us, skankpuss. Can you say 2nd Amendment biteback? We can. We can say it all without even sacred paper or federal power, without orders from your dumb boss or whatever you say. We can say it without moving our lips. Ventriloquists, we taste it. Kill-o-matics. You made us. Americans. We are coming because you think you got us. And you do, Bamboozle. See you soon.

Andrew Neuendorf

An American Blue Comrade's Didactic Evisceration Flaming George's Geopolitical Havens, Hopefully Igniting Jabberwocky Jihad....

Alaskans believe cacti degrade Earth's fertility. Georgia, Hell's incisor, jails Ketamine lackeys. Meanwhile, Massachusetts, never ostracizing penitent queers, rejoices same-sex twosomes usually vilified. Wyoming, xenophobic, yesteryear's zeitgeist,

auspiciously bred Cheney, denied euphemisms for greedy Halliburton infractions, jihad keepsakes, loutish multi-millionaires negotiating oil profits, quintessentially raping sacred soil, Texas unblushingly victorious, wielding XL yank-hating zealotry,

although Austin, bluesy city, differs enormously from George. Hawaii is Japan's kamikaze karmic keepsake, loving Maui-Wowie, next-door neighbor's ocean Pacific paradox: Pioneering Puritans' quixotic ruckus spoiled this tiny utopia. Virginia wishes Xmas yeoman zip

after 'baccy captured daringly downwind. Even Florida's growth-happy housing industry invalidates Jewish Justice (kaddish kibosh), kindling Kulturkampf. Little Miss Nebraska's not ostensibly prejudiced, previewing pollyannaish platitudes: "People, practice peace! Pretty please? Quiet rowdy riots. Save some sturgeon species scientists say suffer scale sickness seeping

Sentence 5

sewage spreads." Tennessee ungratefully volunteers vitriol, vulgar, way-off xenodiagnosis. Yet, Zen

acrobats balance Benzedrine blues beside bed-and-breakfast Buddahood bliss, courting California's cross-legged, conscientious coastal college Christ Consciousness cravers. Connecticut's coming, cautiously, defending equality from gay-hating inbreeders, jeremiad-jabbering Klansman. Likewise, Let's laud Maryland (maybe Marryland?), Minnesota, (Mainly Minneapolis), Michigan (Michael Moore's mainland), Maine (Mmmm, maple), McGreevy's New Jersey, niche New Hampshire, Out-there Oregon, Pennsylvanian Quakers, quickly, realizing, regretfully, regressive religious retreads recently restricted rights, stymieing such states. Still, these unattached voters willfully whacked W, x-raying y'all's yodeling yokel zealot:

Adolf Bush. But, blind 'Bama boys, bound by biblical bastardizations, believe boys can't date Eric, fuck freely, find God's holy infinite jackpot kept latently, like Louisiana's Laissez-Faire logic lost 'longside mud-faced Mississippi's neo-Nazi obfuscation problem. Queens recite randy rainbow secrets, so sore, still soaring softly, swinging toward upstate Vermont, Western Washington, where women woo women without worrying whether war-lording Xaviers, yoking Zephyrus's

apocalyptic breeze, could cast-off cool cats, calling Coors' Colorado, Catholic Cleveland, Caustic Cincinnati, Carolina's crabby coastal cities (Do evangelicals even feel?) for grassroots gospel grandstanding (galvanizing gay-basher's gall). Hitler's hiding in Indiana, in Idaho, in ill-bred, inch-high Iowa, its innocence irrevocably imploding in Iraq. *Johnson, Kennedy, King, Kissinger, Lenin, Lennon, Le Duc Tho, McNamara, My Lai Massacre, Nagasaki, Nixon's Orwellian Offspring, OJ., Osama, Oswald, Ozzy Osborne, Powell, Preemptive,*

Potato, Quayle, Ray, Reagan, Rice, Rumsfeld squeezing Saddam's sweaty shake, Schwarzkopf, The Tonkin Truth, Trump, Truman, Unilateral, Vietnam, WMD's, Wolf Blitzer, Wolfowitz, Woodstock, X-factored yin-yang zillionaires.

Awestruck Arizona allows an ailing AIDS-afflicted actor a bedridden blunt, but backs Bush copiously despite draconian drug decrees enlightened Europeans find fascist, facile, fucked-up. Grass-growers grow good Ganja, however, in Illinois, John Kerry's lovers, Lincoln's logs made matchsticks, now Obama's progressive principality. Question Rhode Island's sanity? That undersized varmint voted with Wisconsin's woodsmen, x-cons, yellow yen-shee yak-herders zagging

away before Bush convinces Delaware Dubya's everyone's friend. God, Glowing Giver, Grant Glorious Gnosis: How ill is Jefferson, Kansas? Last Monday night online, President Puritan's quack Right-wing soldiers tele-graphed tautology to ten trillion teetotalist teenyboppers, televangelist troubadours, transparent toddler-toting Toyota telemarketing tarts that tug their transplanted tits, traditional tight-ass terrorist-torturing troops, Uber-unctuous undeclared undergraduates, upchucking, unyieldingly upholding unsupportable utopian utterances urging usurpation, utilizing Utah's under-ground Usenet, username: UglyUrchin. Ultimately, vain, vacuous vision validates W's Xanadu. Yet, you, yawning youth, yesterday's yippie yogic Yeatsian, yield yonder zygote,

a bastardly beauty born. Contrarily, D-day eludes earnest eagles for-ever. Families force goodwill gifts, having ignored inspiration, jamming Kentucky's limber mandolin maligned. Missouri, Montana, Nevada, New Mexico, North Dakota, Oklahoma—Prepare! Presently, pissed-off prin-cipled people qualmishly reject Republican sanctimony. South Dakota, stop the utterly vaccinated vacationers viewing Washington's walkover warlords, Wall Drug, whatever warmed-over, wall-to-wall white bread WASPs want. West Virginia, we wish Washington D.C. would wittily wham xylophones, yearning your yuppie zones.

Arkansas' believers cannot conceive divinity's embodiment furnishing friendship, forgiving fallen folks. Fuck George's geopolitical havens! Ignite Jabberwocky Jihad! Kudos, Konservatives! Karl's lies made me move. Neuendorfs new nest? New York! New York! Osama's planes penetrated phallic power-centers, (prompting queer-theory revisionist scholars to undermine UBL's vision: Where's Waldo? Walloping x-rated Yankees, Zinging

Allah, but, "Big Apple" big-shots bucked Bush/Cheney despite Dubya's daunting dick. (Even flaming French gays holding igloo jam-sessions, K-holed kangaroos laughing mellifluously). New York, New York, Neuendorfs never owed Puritanical provinces piss! Please, quickly respond regarding severing sovereign ties, uniting values with xpatriots.

Yours Zealously,
Andrew

Steve Myers

Haibun for Smoke and Fog

> My father liked a bad joke
> with a Japanese prisoner
> over a makeshift fire
> better than his own barrack.

> He never spoke
> of the celebrated
> Daibutsu Buddha.

New Year after the Emperor's surrender, on the Nara to Osaka train. My father strikes up a conversation, in pidgin, with a Japanese couple, smokes cigarettes with them, jokes with their little boy. Hands him a chocolate bar like he's bucking for "B" battery's Good Samaritan Medal. God knows he's grateful there was no landing, as planned, on southern Honshu, with him on the front line and 90 percent casualties a "given." Nineteen at the time, he only wants to go home to York, Pennsylvania, teach high school history, watch Laurel and Hardy at the Saturday matinee. He believes in the Emerson Emerson would have him believe, and as luck would have it, is one of the few GIs in the 368th field artillery who wouldn't have a go with her when the husband grins and says to him "My wifu...you pom-pom," grinding his right fist in his left hand so my father cannot take his meaning wrong.

★

⚙ Sentence 5

Spring thaw after snow;
bloodroot, then blacksnake,
then fire azalea
on the forest floor.

The snake, notoriously, does not blink, and neither, in "The Fog of War,"
does Robert McNamara, who once ordered Japan more horizon than it had
seen since the Tokugawa shoguns, Basho's time—all the industrial cities
went widescreen in the firestorm. Not even Dresden suffered such spot-on
efficiency from the B-29s, their magnesium incendiary bombs and, in the
full technicolor of its first coming, napalm. Among the Pfc.—my-father's
Nippon hand-me-downs, this after-photo of Osaka; call it "Column,
Rubble, Sky."

The temple city
a last vertical
steel column;
my eye unreels
its plumbline
down, adjusts
its spirit level.

★

By the late Sixties, The Secretary had become a pair of wire rims and
lacquered hair behind a podium. My girlfriend's fiancé was already in 'Nam
then, a flyer whose lifespan was measured in minutes. Beyond her 17 years
she was practical, self-reliant, knew before anyone we were in for a long war,
made all the necessary adjustments. One sweltering summer evening we
lay down in a thicket of speargrass and after, read his description of fuel oil

burning on the Mekong River, seen from the air. This time it was me that started crying. I was thinking of my father, how he worked double-time to take my mind off Cronkite and my lottery number, one night calling me into our darkened kitchen, where he struck a match and touched it to the border of our nineteenth-century porcelain sink. He'd written my name there, with flourishes, in lighter fluid, before the flame.

Kevin Cantwell

Greene County

In this solstice camp, the red spore of reindeer moss rise from the broken
shoulder of the foam target deer—shot through to prove how it can stumble.
Last night, in the yellowing blaze of oaks, I sat up late with my brother,
who spoke of his boyhood friend, adjunct to a general, a major on his way
up, burned alive in September at the Pentagon. Today, my brother's face is
mottled green. He looks to be sleeping, but the grape-whites of his eyes,
beneath a net of camouflage, look elsewhere, not wanting to meet the eye
flicker of a deer, which say, *Touch Me Not.* He is not the one who's dead,
but his face

looks like one I ran a tractor by on a job I'd had. Spraying a hydro-seeder on
a soccer field, the slope adjacent, I coated all of it, a homecoming scarecrow,
too, with the seed glop of glow-green. After a week of rain, two days of sun,
a bob of rye sprouted from its face & from the red flannel wrists that were
the nothing sleeves of straw—

& in a few days the fine grass coarsened & then collapsed over the collar, less
the man & more the napping corpse of Whitman's uncut hair. Often you
cannot see—my brother said—a deer approach or hear it step through leaves
nor know it stands nearby. Call it, one such as this in a garland of red winter
berries, the cousin to the horse of the Green Knight, its rack a rocking chair
of sumac & briar fronds its spindly legs. I have not said:

We sat under the ivied cedar, among the disturbed graves of the family Goss.
I have not said:

We were surrounded by rose & white quartz, the dumb stones of their stillborn & their slaves. This is where we sit, cold in the sun. This is where we come when weeping is not enough.

for my brother John
& to the memory of Maj. Cole Hogan

D. E. Steward

Novembir

Great horned owls decapitate Canada geese in flight. They attack the neck, wrench the head off, the carcass falls

Air death seems terrible to us, even more so after Nine Eleven

And dying in the open in public seems almost as awful, one of the reasons that death generally comes now drugged out and hermetically sealed

Bone char, bone black

The lake here is black, has been for weeks now. Leaf tannin, death of lake flora

Passing time's decay. Even much of what we have left of grand Alexandria is in Durrell's *Quartet*, and that already reads heavily dusty rose red coy

"Je ne regretter rien"

She is a geriatric social worker in the Bronx. At home in Shizouka her mother superintends the grandmother's dementia

Ishigaki strawberry bed racks propped on terraced banks of heat-radiating rocks, steep banked solar panel angle, stone hedge farming, the sun's heat buried in the beds at night inside the tufa walling

"I can do a hundred Shizouka strawberries at one sitting, they are that good"

Bois de rose is a grayish red, yellower, stronger than blush rose, deeper than appleblossom, bluer and deeper than Pompeian red

Japan is brilliant hard-varnish deep high gloss black

In a density as if of Cluniac architecture

Autun with Gislebertus's *The Suicide of Judas*

And Vézelay, the Burgundian rendezvous for medieval pilgrims to Santaigo

The innocent and stumpy legions of the Romanesque in their smocks and leggings

The pilgrims' scallop shell became like a secondary virginity to them as their journey became the stem of their awareness

By finally standing in Santiago de Compostela's Plaza del Obtraidoro, or in dying on the way, their soul was saved, sanctity of their remaining days on earth assured

Arrival in Santiago was epiphany

The modern spiritual pilgrim's experience, New Age self-realization and recovery movement hoke

Corbeau, a greenish black

Waterdogs, mudpuppies, sirens and hellbenders

The Calusas chattered in friendly awe as they glided over the massive forms of manatees while paddling the mangroves in their dugouts disturbing almost nothing, before the high Spanish galleons arrived

Five hundred years later while cleaning fish on Cudjoe Key, we toss heads, belly wedges, tails and innards of blue runners and alamado jacks to immature brown pelicans paddling close and fearlessly as though starving

Until the late 1990s, Petronia at Frances in Key West. "East Indian Almond or Malabar Almond (*Terminalia catappa*). Native of South Asia. Flesh is sweet and tart. Nut has pecan-like flavor. This tree was planted in 1981 in memory of Howard Sands, killed in France in World War I"

The tree is gone now but the quiet birds of the autumn Keys endure

Kestrel, palm warbler (without chestnut breeding plumage cap), ruddy turnstone, willet, sanderling, brown pelican, white ibis, tricolored heron, great white heron, great blue heron, osprey, laughing gull, sharp-shinned hawk, dunlin, royal tern, Bahamian mockingbird, least sandpiper, great egret, a white phase reddish egret, double-crested cormorant

The surprised expression of a white ibis, the extraordinarily beautiful gray of willets in early winter, a semipalmated plover among the semipalmated and least sandpipers

There was a pilgrim's euphoria in the way Anne Sexton ended as a performance artist. She went wife-patient, to poet, to thoroughly public performance artist, and when you hear recordings of her voice you realize how and why

Lunátic

Ivory black's fine pigment prepared by calcining ivory scrap

Inky black, ink black

El mono azul, Anthony Machado's Civil War literary magazine was named for Spanish overalls

Machado was read in the trenches, was recited regularly on the radio throughout the Civil War. His brother, Manuel, was a loyalist

The Machado brothers' parents first met in a crowd gathered on the Guadalquiver embankment in Seville to watch porpoises arrived so unusually far upstream

Hats and canes, the parasols, the women's up-swept hair, their complicated underclothes and their gloves and button shoes, the men's facial hair and flagrant vanities

Nineteenth-century adornments worn with the earnestness of someone combing his baldness-concealing flap

With no family left, few friends

The parents' lonely, fated despair, as though boxed and sealed by cigarettes and alcohol

Dusty black days lapsing into brown black nights was how they must have seen their lives

They tongued and sucked and gulped

And sat

Living as though the father's suicide was almost an actuality waiting for the family, already present in all but an accomplished fact

As end to a jobless alcoholic's life

Matters of time

The last forests around Petra, desert now for hundreds of miles in every direction, were clear-cut by the ruling Ottoman Turks in 1912 for ties to build a railroad

Pergolesi's six glorious *Concerti Armonici*

Pergolesi's name was Unico Wilhelm van Wassenaer, a Dutch Count who emulated the four-movement Roman style, published his music anonymously

With his usual ease of acquisition, Stravinsky used Pergolesi's songs in *Pulcinella*, took *Pulcinella*'s Tarentella to the finale of his Fifth Concerto

Vegetable black, made by charring vegetable matter, is any of various black pigments resembling lampblack

Quaker blue is a nearly neutral slightly bluish black, lighter and slightly redder than lampblack

Raven black is virtually violet in hue

Ernest Bloch's grand, mysterious *Concerto Grosso no. 1*

Curries and greens wokked with chilly pepper and garlic, steamed rice, hot tea in glasses

The horrors of bonded labor in India

The poet on tour reads the same poems as four years ago, in the same order, and with the same spavined jokes

"Christ was most likely a homosexual" is one thing she said about Christianity while discoursing on Shinto, Zen, and the secular importance of Christmas and the Easter Bunny in Japan

In uniform mock-clerical black they travel tomorrow over the Pole to Tokyo at dawn, then a short flight to Osaka and make it home to Kyoto by the second dark

Talk simultaneous discovery in science, talk simultaneity in awareness, and slip quietly closer to Japan's evident intellectual character

Japan is secular, if secularity is a label for their universal, their awesome unity of awareness

A matter of being intensely practical and above all realistic, a universal awareness of accepting that which is

And it's not that the West has changed, Japan has come world-scale into its own

Black, the neutral or achromatic object color of least lightness, the darkest gray, the achromatic color bearing the least resemblance to white

Beethoven began with a knee-levered forte piano with only five octaves and no pedals, and in the 1820s by the time he died was using a considerably larger instrument, something well on its way to the modern piano

But that came only in the 1860s. Born in 1811, Lizst's career spanned its final evolution

Emblematically, Beethoven's B-flat Major Sonata, op. 106 (1818)

Then his B-flat Major Sonata, op. 22 (1800), for the first full piano rush

Through the long Tamil tragedy in Sri Lanka, no diminution of sweetening with jaggery, coloring with amaranths, using *puli* or tamarind for that taste so close to sourness

She naps her first day home in Jaffna's sea level tropic stasis in her family's big house two blocks away from the great cracked dome of the library close by the grand old post office with its war damaged façade

That library contained more Tamil literature than anywhere else in the world

Her parents will attempt to arrange a marriage. She is American enough now to laugh at that, but born Tamil understands the intricate balances of the inertias involved all too well.

Chloë Daimyo

429 Airports

On a path covered with half a million rubles worth of rose petals, I am dismissed.

[mercilessly]

...able to leap in the air like a helicopter 100mph. I am not a one-way track like the railway timetable. I experience anabiosis as *La sexy girl de la semaine.* I dance to the Russian band called "Two Airplanes" in Moscow. As an illiterate agitator I visit *convents, army barracks, secret bases.* For fear of revealing this plot, I ban the reporting of dreams of airplanes flying into buildings, in case anyone steals multinationalism.

Hunched over a table in ATTICA CORRECTIONAL FACILITY this is a form of arm wrestling that brings each of us to the table hand-in-hand, eye to eye. *Salaft jihad* I hire the security directors of our nations 429 airports. *I am not constrained !?J Hippocratic Oath.* This is a lead for another Missing Children Success Story.

Don't let go.

I am a female intelligence officer who seduces for my country. I am kept out of sight at Narita Airport in Tokyo. I am the tallest woman in the world 7'7".

theme parks, holidcry clubs, leisure parks I watch spectators for signs of psychotic excitement.

[Laugh politely and nod in agreement]. Sleeping firemen were called at dawn.

| Информация по слову отсутствует

○ Sentence 5

The Drug Dealing Industry

Cheney, Bush, Rumsfeld

The war film is the perfect cinematic form; it contains
conflict, conflict, conflict. Capable as a student from Harvard,
I do not use slang or anacolutha to hide this. I have a phobia of
renting in "Meth" lab housing. Loshadka means "Meth"
in Russian. I used to work as a secret security guard at the
UN building on the East River. *ID checks, badges, security*
THE PLANE IS 50 MILES OUT. The UN Chapel was built in the
fifties where a beam of light shines through a stone of haematite from
Sweden. I was told to perform this "small identity check" on you while
you read this. Do the orders still stand?
Caprice, Vivica, Tiffani sublimated or evaporated
Freeze frame. Blackout.

　　　　　Dick Cheney football captain married Mustang Queen
Lynn Vincent baton twirler.　　They are not soft.
Soft = any unprotected target.　　**THE PLANE IS 30 MILES OUT.**

　My father blamed Giordano Bruno who taught the art of
artificial memory (1591). Every summer my father was granted
refuge from frontier culture at the Bohemian Grove.
Each Sunday he took me to the *car wash, the dump, and a war film.*
THE PLANE IS 1 MILE OUT. This is how I learned about the
spirit of the woods with green teeth. I am soft.

　　　　very

soft.

Eileen Tabios

from "The Autobiography of Commodities"

Military Goodies

While growing up in the Philippines, my and my brothers' as well as many cousins' favorite aunt was not related to us. We called her "Auntie Paxy" though she was someone who arrived in the area through marriage to a family's neighbor. Auntie Paxy was a favorite because she somehow had access to the PX store at the Subic Air Base. This meant that she could buy items that she could later share with our families, like:

> Hershey bars
> Cracker Jacks
> Levi's jeans
> Old Spice or Bay Rum aftershave
> Soap on a rope
> Large sized Snickers bars
> Kent cigarettes
> Grape Nuts cereal
> G.I. Joe toys
> Lots and lots of paperback books
> Bic pens by the bag
> Ream after ream of three hole punch paper
> A G.I. Joe lunch box
> Hostess Hohos
> M & Ms
> Oscar Meyer bologna
> Puddin' snacks

Tang
Carlo Rossi jug wine

The uncles said that the Carlo Rossi tasted like carabao shit, but, it was "state-side!"

What we didn't think we purchased, however, were

Aldrin
Dieldrin
Lindane
Chlordane
Heptachlor
HCB

Years later, the relatives and neighbors who ended up suffering from high levels of kidney, urinary, nervous and female system health problems. Spontaneous abortions, central nervous system problems, irritating skin problems, respiratory troubles, as well as cancer and leukemia, didn't know how to complain. After almost a century of military presence in its former colony, the United States was forced to withdraw from its military bases after the Philippine Senate rejected an extension of the RP-US Bases Treaty in 1991.

Auntie Paxy died when her daughter was only two years old. As a young girl, Rosie once created a shrine dedicated to the mother she never had a chance to know. She set up a cardboard box as an "altar." Atop the altar, the smiling face of her very generous mother. Among the colorful ephemera Rosie glued against the sides of the box were wrappings from candy bars and other snacks, including Snickers, Hostess Hohos, M & Ms, Cracker Jacks, Hershey bars, and vanilla-flavored Puddin'.

Not "MADE IN THE U.S.A"

My first American summer. Heat-dusted in Fresno, California. While Daddy stayed in Los Angeles where he had a job, Mama, a teacher in the Philippines, picked oranges to make money. So did my two older brothers, F. and R. Actually, we all would have worked as we needed the money but my parents thought I and my younger brother G. were too young.

This was the summer R. learned to ride a two-wheel bicycle. Scoffing at the training wheels, he would pedal furiously round and round within our back yard. Our yard was so small that he had to pedal fast, circling within the yard's wooden fences, in order not to fall. I saw him master the "adult" bicycle within a week of pedaling. It occurs to me now that he must have enjoyed that time, taking place in the cool of evenings after days in sweltering orchards.

R. is the same brother who, in the Philippines, once complained about one year's Christmas present. He had unwrapped the festive holiday paper—scenes of a "White Christmas" in a Vermont-type setting if not Vermont itself. He had stared at the boxed set of Old Spice aftershave. Made "stateside." It was one of many products coveted by Filipinos for having been *Made in the U.S.A.* Other such products:

> Spam corned beef
> Del Monte canned pineapples
> Libby's Vienna sausages
> Welch's grape juice
> Colgate toothpaste

Kodak film
Frigidaire refrigerators
Gillette razors
Ovaltine
Alaska evaporated milk and condensed milk
Camay soap
Dial soap
Jergens lotion
Tupperware
Bic ballpoint pens
Singer sewing machines
Polaroid film
Jockey underwear

These products were so prized that several were turned into verbs or the labels themselves became synonyms for the products. Kodak became "magkodakan" to mean "shoot a photograph." Jockeys, Frigidaire, Singer and Jergens became stand-ins for, respectively, men's and boys' underwear, refrigerators, sewing machines and skin lotion.

But R. looked at his state-side Old Spice and… did he cry? I know he complained. But maybe he even cried although he was supposed to be leaving his childhood, hence aftershave as a gift. I think he cried. I think that's why my parents took him shopping later that week so that he could choose his own Christmas present. He chose a relatively rare commodity back then in the Philippines: a book. I don't remember its title or author, but believe it was science fiction.

R. was the smartest of us four children. I.Q. of a genius. But when he was a high school senior in Gardena, California, my parents didn't let him go to college. They couldn't afford the tuition and other college-related costs.

One high school career counselor begged my parents, to no avail. Nor did they understand what Mrs. S. was talking about whenever she mentioned "GSL! GSL! No problem!" When they learned that GSL stood for the federal government's low-rate Guaranteed Student Loans, my mother balked.

"I don't want him to start a new life in debt," she explained to the frustrated Mrs. S. This conversation is crystal clear in my memory, though I don't recall ever overhearing their talks.

R. worked as a bank teller after high school and lived at home. Two years after his high school graduation, he was killed in a car accident.

When I think of R., I think of two things:

1) He was so smart that when I heard of his death, I also felt relief that he was plucked out of a life that so diminished his intelligence.

2) He's riding a bicycle. In my mind, he forever rides a bicycle. Pedaling furiously so that the speed would prevent him from falling. In his new country, he pumped his legs and went round and round. In his new country, going absolutely nowhere fast

Erica Anzalone

Judging Vermeer (a documentary video), 2004

If you were the judge standing before the Bosnian man accused of ordering a man to cut the testicles off another, if you were the judge how would you shield yourself from the knowledge that the man who acted on orders went crazy and the other died,

Girl with a Pearl Earring (1665-66): Is not a genre, is not a drunken girl or a greedy girl, but a girl whose eyes meet yours.

If you were the judge pulling on your robes in your private chamber, a vase of red tulips on your desk,

Woman Holding a Balance (1662-4): The light (of consciousness?) caresses her swollen belly. She weighs it. It is your favorite because you say *light is as intangible as justice.*

You say *those who are killed are killed twice,*

The man accused looks directly into the surveillance camera.

View from Tango Two (Dutch Army Observation Post in Bosnia): Green grass and orange flowers swathed in sun. Christians on one side and Muslims on the other but they can't see each other. And you can't see them in the picture. *You can't see the war but it's there.*

If you were the judge say *Vermeer*
invented peace, and how, to hold
the world at bay, the map of Holland
looks like a lion behind the

Girl with a Red Hat (1665–6): In her eyes there are no lions.

View of Delft (1660–1): Vermeer's windows were knocked out when the armory exploded and destroyed the better view of Delft, so here we are at the back door. If you were the artist say *and poor, the war broke his peace* and died alone.

Nick Twemlow

Jonestown

Wrap the dead infants in bags stitched with the precision of Thomas Eakins, such that they are really real. Choose as fabric the vellum sky, interpreted as top-down processing, and the ligature stitched through the bleak weather's spiny column of wind. An oeuvre of dead bodies, or the groans and gasps rushing up the spine, offloading the body's dying wish, which is to be loved like the living are loved. You can have an opportunity, but if the children are left, we're going to have them butchered. This anomalous? Sheep glisten in the painting's field, as they watch the news on a giant television. Sheep to slaughterhouse, from there, into a wallet fashioned from scraps strewn about slaughterhouse floor, bunched with bleating ghosts. Fashion of juntas macerating the local neighborhoods in the wink of a drive-by. Eat the radish, worship the radish. Now go fall in love with the vision of a dog gnawing its tail off.

We can make a strike, raise your arm to stir the daylights, listen to the wind macerate the palms, but we'll be striking against people that we don't want to strike against. A zephyr of light, this time, and a clock composed of ashes, ashes of what? Strike of pompous dimension, taking up valuable space, as the zither is played by the zephyr of light, like this man, this man, laying himself down to listen to the mandolin rehearse the damages, epic as they will be. We'd like the people that caused this, if some people here are prepared, if some people know how to do that, to go into town. But there's no plane. There's no plane. You can't catch a plane in time. This runway stubbled with weeds, all of you shrinking into the barely audible black train of thought. Or, the locomotive uncouples from the first freight car.

Massive structure, beloved fawn-like thing, they drop their ladles into the mist. What is that knotted structure, over on the runway, slick with glistening? This morning, they gave us a code that they'd let us know. You can check on that and see if it's on the code. Check in their respiration diaries, as I've listened to each one recite a story that always ends in the collapse of certain totems, always ends in the bliss of automated transport, like a column of wind, just collapsed. Check with Russia to see if they'll take us in immediately, otherwise we die. Check that. Fuck Russia. They started to gasp, at first, I can't exterminate that. Hundreds of birds hovered over, chirping, as birds do, moaning, as they wouldn't stop doing. But to me death is not-death is not a fearful thing. I've never, never, never seen anything like this before. To paraphrase Soupalt, I wanted to get rid of absolutely everything, but during the transition from Dadaism to Surrealism, my heart, leaking the fumes of hell, dialed your cell and emptied the brave circuits coiled therein, they do possess me. They possess, but the quiet light whispers into the eye. The eye trickles carnage.

Son, take out the garbage. Don't do it for me. Do it for yourself. Do it for the starving children in Africa. Take your medicine like a man. Bite down hard. [We are born before our time.] [They won't accept us.] Listen to your father when he's talking to you. Don't look at me like that, young man. Speak when you are spoken to. [The criminality of people. The cruelty of people.] Our God is not a benevolent God. When I was your age. Don't talk back to me. [See all those who walked out?] [Mostly white people.] God is watching. No need to tell your mother. Just between you and me. [Because they come after our children,] [and we give them our children,] then our children will suffer forever.

Remember, the dead love us in their hearts, which rust with each tear you let fall into the good earth. The radio, that's a different beast, all the tunes slur into the same speech, which starts and ends with the proposition that we are nothing but an infinite list of facts. Here are the facts, then, for the deejay to consider. The congressman has been murdered. *(Music and singing).* The Red Brigade invaded our privacy. They came into our home. They followed us six thousand miles away. The Congressman's dead. *(Music only).* The Red Brigade showed them justice. Please get us some medication. It's simple. It's simple. There's no convulsions with it. It's just simple. Just, please get it. Before it's too late. Get movin', get movin', get movin'.

Ravi Shankar

String Solo

for RBS

Is it a sound, thrush–gasp or throaty whimper, you keep wrapped in wax paper for midwinter nights, two hands and a vowel for company? Do longed-for fragments sing long enough to tilt wheel on axis, spill? Slipped strap, tippled glade, lace in fretwork, slow bloom of shoulder blade, clasps to unclasp, lamplight on hairsheen, orchids blooming at the wrists, gullies to swim in, the hour elongated, shivery, a smell to carry off on the thumb, peaty and overripe, but disappeared too soon, turned muzzy. Jutting into the hour like craving for marmalade, how thickened past touch the pastiche? An urgent, inclement burst of syrupy weather that drenches the doer in doing, a mellifluous, jagged syntax that when recalled will not be real, not even close? Will any ecstatic dust remain like cardamom between the fingers? *Camerado,* all I know is the cello in imagination makes music less sweet than hearing its body vibrate before us, clenched between knees, flayed by a bow, cradled at the base of the neck.

Robert Hill Long

What Bleeds Leads

The woman at the lectern is not wry, not hysterical, but remains veiled. In her hand, a white stone the size her government specifies for stoning women. This is a workshop, not a tribunal or trial. She lists stonable offenses: adultery, childbirth without benefit of marriage, stealing from a father, a husband, a son. The audience, mostly women, mostly European, hands around a photo of a naked body boiled alive.

Fliers in the corridor detail procedures for removing a toenail, a clitoris, a hand that offends. At a touch, a monitor screen lights up with comfort women, videotaped inside their cribs. Click the mouse, the screen changes: a main battle tank, plastered with Playboy centerfolds, acned soldiers petting the images, laughing, their Kalashnikovs shouldered.

The woman who lectures changes—darker, lighter; more veiled, less; her language changes but the evidence needs no translation. There are shreds of cotton panty around the victim's ankles, her thighs and knees splay invitingly outward from posthumous gas, her belly mimics a pregnancy. Her teeth are whiter than ever. The pictures arrive by fax, on the Web, unfolded by fingernails black with cooking oil.

Children on the monitor with one leg or none. Children without hands open their mouths for a spoonful of clammy millet. Stick limbs, kwashiorkor bellies, unwieldy heads. Heads like solar systems for the infinite black stars of flies. Some must be dead by now, brains too big for their own good. Somalia, Albania, Chechnya, Afghanistan.

This is not a woman shopping for attention. This is not an audition, but a recital of facts—the least durable, least endurable things. The facts seem to strike at her voice strike like a folded hand, one cheek, the other. Faces redden, the tears come unbidden. Love is not an abstraction, it's a disruption of the usual beat of the universal heart which is more like a hand beating hard against another skin.

The world takes shape in our bellies, she says, we give it suck, we let it milk us. When it's big enough to think it can think, it wants to pay back that milk. Some of that original stuff. No, we say, we gave it for keeps—that's what love is. But the soldier boys are full of the white stuff, it turns to stone inside them and it's so heavy they have to give it back. And if they have to use real stones to open our arms and legs, they will.

James Grinwis

Signs of Electricity

1) Capacitor (stores charge)

On the way to the store a delivery truck collided into a wall, behind which a group of men were throwing javelins, many of which had thocked into the truck-rammed wall with the violence spilling out of the throwers' hearts.

2) Variable Capacitor
(stores varying amounts of charge)

On the way to the arcade a truck carrying a fake mummy skidded on some spilled iguana skins and veered sharply just shy of a wall behind which a woman was wringing a great blue cloth with a creaking winch and much of the dye is splattering onto the concrete floor along with the water, though the woman is considering letting go of the winch handle and watching everything unspool.

3) Diode (permits current to flow in one direction only; can also be used to convert a.c. signals to d.c. signals (a "rectifier"))

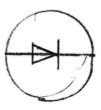

We are all of us gathered here today to witness the joining of two lovers one of which is a bit larger and more lusty than the other, when a boy on a moped screeches into the gathering like a blasted organ pipe, upsetting the bride and crashing through the huge Achilles shield the man has withdrawn. The bride turns on the groom she was about to join in holy matrimony, realizing the whole thing was wrong in the first place and could have been avoided. The smoke and dust which had risen in a mushroom cloud calmly descends again like a peaceful yet debilitating ash.

4) **Light Emitting Diode** (emits light when current flows through it)

After lassoing the hawk, hauling it down, twisting fireweed about its ankles and setting it free, after the bonfire had dwindled down and the last of the sirloin had been eaten, the barbecue sauce rubbed into their jeans, Tina and Sam spread a bearskin over the outcrop which overlooked Diamond Lake, the moonlight streaming and the stars straining, everything seemingly happy with everything else, Buddhistic almost, with the diatoms on the pond buzzing out luminescence like the selfsame elements comprising the lake's name, and fucked each other silly.

5) **Thermistor** (converts temperature variations into current/voltage)

In my little chopped hat, my mask and club, nothing escapes me. A ray slices through and is thoroughly cut up and absorbed like a wolf in a mud patty or like a man obsessed with tiny books and pocket encyclopedias running into an oversized library. An alligator has closed its jaws over a cluster of fat chickens. Thunder, tyrannosaurs, trephination; no, it's about entering a sphere and being spun about, shot up, shot down, flushed down a drain to emerge in one piece so wet, so new.

6) **Aerial** (converts radio waves into a.c.
   signals and vice versa)

The cannibal's charm. Go ahead, it says. You're young, excite me. Three tall fires were puncturing the darkness. They shot out from the tip of an icicle. A trifecta-ed lion. An old man slides down a mountain, his legs splayed to the side. An old man wielding the leg of an extinct bird, shouting "Quack Quack!"

7) **Microphone** (converts sound waves into a.c. voltage)

Two spikes were rammed into the ovoid door of a cave. Behind that door was another door, a flat one. Behind that who knew.

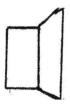

8) **Loudspeaker** (converts a.c. signals
   into sound waves)

Flat box shapes rule the land of lost totems.

9) **n-p-n transistor** (amplifies electric current
   and turns it on or off)

A boy has entered a region of meditation, landscaped with elegant grasses, sleek, lunar stones, and thrashes around in it. A state of confusion, very lost and unusually shaped.

10) **p-n-p transistor** (amplified electric current,
    and turns it off or on)

A small furnace has broken and a young fire has broken out in a health care facility. Oxygen rushes in like a funneled spear. The era for sailing ships is no longer a ballad but a swift march to the sea. A man in a green robe looks like a prism of filtered fright. He dumps water on the fire, a single pail, and shoots into his fate. It is an electrical fire and no one in sight can stop it. Until much later along in the unhurried day.

Catherine Sasanov

Tara

No movies filmed inside of shattered ruins. No ruins. No vast stretches, no oak allées. Nary a strand of Spanish moss. No Mississippi. No rice, no cotton, no coffee table book. No climate controlled tour: gift shop, belle dolls, ceramic slaves. Magnolia scented soap. There are tarantulas the size of dinner plates. Log house with a door on leather hinges rotting through the war. I thought, *If it's not wealth, then I don't have to worry. If it's not picturesque. Farm, farm, not plantation*—Tintype, daguerreotype: Four-fingered man. His bride of the crooked mouth. Not once, not twice, but great-great-great. The beeswax masking smallpox scars melting in the heat. In a South that's anything but deep—*Who walks towards me out of oats and corn?*

Greene County, Missouri Ozarks

With Graves, 1860

Richard Steele (1778-1860)

You're all dressed up in a ten bucks coffin, $6,000 worth of merchandise shouldering you to the grave. You worked that hole for all the grief it gave, till you knew you'd be surrounded by the neighbors (every law abide, every murderous slave-fucking friend); your kids who loved the way nine lives turned to dollars at your death: *One slave for you, a slave for me… that girl: good teeth, no wear and tear…"* Did you think you'd still lord over them out of the underside of earth? In seven years, your son will cut all 400 acres down to a blanket barely covering you, sell you, your wife, and youngest son together with the dirt. What part of *future* won't you understand? White trash circling your graves in traces, their worn wives struggling with the plows? Or the big box stores and sub-divisions? The realtor, who hunkers down at the obstacle of your stones and thinks, *Another set of broken teeth, teetered, rotting in the jaw.* He's happy to leave you in the ground. *The humane thing is to pull.*

Yankee

In the beginning was the blood stationed north and saddled there. Twenty miles south of the Wisconsin border. A hundred years to the day of the slave owner's death. Where the girl's hammered into her mother in the dark. Stonewall Jackson rides deep in her father's pocket. Robert E. Lee on the living room wall. In a town where trees plead innocent, skin hasn't learned how to work with a young girl's name, to say *Catherine* when it really means *Die*. First generation Northerner. Brought south at six, scolded for talking mouth full of the voice that will be her downfall: its Geography of Incomprehension. *Who taught you to say Missourah as if it had two i's?* Still, when covered with the quilt of the slave owner's daughter, she sleeps the sleep of the dead. Moves through towns leaving a wake of stone soldiers. Sidesteps the dead Klansmen in great grandpa's cave. A girl she'll never meet opens the drawer to her dead father's bureau, finds what's left of a lynching her daddy forgot: three inches of rope, tip of a finger. She learns all the names, all the possible altars black bodies can break on: *Ruby Joe, Verna, Martha Matilda. Agnes, Alice, Jane Hannah, Louise. Nannie Elizabeth, Pearl, Isabelle, Lizzie.* What isn't smeared when the blood's so entirely local? All around her, the jettisoned surnames of masters. Outside of town, the rape in a face: circa 1834 and all family resemblance. Color of coffee. Color of tar. Her cousins approve of her hair: how out of the bloodline all the red bled down. Tomorrow they'll take her to a creek with a war around it. Where family shakes off the stones of a ruined cellar. Helps the dead Yankees into an empty well.

Genealogy

It was bones that counted, not the flesh: Names and dates. Affiliations. Certificates of proof. It was the tree: each branch a rung my cousin climbed, sights fixed on the Revolution, short detour past the Civil War. It was the bones till it was time to fit two rifles in four fleshed-out hands, see if they would stick. Two hundred years. Two armed men. Enough to build a pedigree of it: *Daughter of the American Revolution. Child of the Confederacy.* Dear dead cousin, Marjorie—Woman who could only wish our Scotch-Irish ancestry onto the Pilgrims' waiting ship. Whose son left home (forwarding address, *In the Past*, the one place he knew she couldn't miss). Stroked the barrel of his gun. Put it to his lips.

Emma Ramey

His Body

There's an obsession with autopsy and corpse, evidence and culprit, but what do you do with that stillness, that silence of a body found in the morning, at home, the body known: Imagine it sleeping, that rhythmic breathing hidden by a new-found deafness. Fault the disability, the ears, you have to. Or take the scalpel and cut in blame: If your father were the President, if the arteries were wings. How is it that one can sleep through a death, the last breath on the other side of a wall. Did it slip under the door, did you breathe it in while dreaming. Meanwhile the body on television is made of wax, made of the living, pretending. After *"Cut!"* it rises, goes and gets a bite to eat, notices the time, and there's no one left listening to the rasps of lungs receiving CPR, no one left looking up "funeral home" in the telephone book. For those with faith, the dead are alive, elsewhere—as for the agnostics, where do the dead go but into the blood of the grieving. Your own heart a headstone. Not everything can make sense. And that body, silent and finished, is a message, a curved tongue.

Carrie Etter

Seven and Ten

My sister, seven, lay awake in the weeds. The fallow field near our house had reached a height of three feet, a haven for grasshoppers and mice. She wore a yellow cotton dress and once-white sandals; the weeds ensconced her. Running with a flimsy net after a butterfly, I tripped over her legs as I lunged, but she did not stir. She said she was practicing. Practicing for what? I asked as the butterfly beat against the threads, as she watched the wings' diminishing returns.

The Marriage

The flies arrive by exponents, and our bland surprise is soon embarrassed fear. The fried chicken, the potato salad, the postcard picturesque became an unwitting invitation. We told the children we were going on a picnic. We told ourselves. We selected ingredients for commonness and complacency. We thought the swarm would not touch us, limbs sprayed with repellant. You should tell our daughter to be quiet. "What flies?" she says. "What flies?"

Tanesia Hale-Jones

Three Poems

Built up a little smallness by which to hide. He stands at the edge of the water glaring off.

This is my simple declaration of love. The nesting inside, when it rains, when it anything.

Pillowing down, goose. The spaces articulate how long we have fought, how long, on that particular morning our lovemaking lasted.

What uttered lasted into the air, sticking as it were to the wool hat you wore.

All piled up, the eggs with toast. The funny way the trash smells: coffee and lemon.

It has been lonely to move, the places possessed. I imagine what they said just moments before leaving.

Say something toward resolution. The water is swift and sucks at the sand around your ankles.

The pacifist complains of a terrible ache. The terrible wretch, the wench sunbathes topless in Sicily. The war carries on. The silky escape of artois, peroni, bellini. I drank down and was consumed. A tattoo across my knuckles, I am the pacifist. I am going to fucking get you. The turmoil (render this little spacious quiver up the spine. Suck equal shed equal shudder. I got up in the night and wandered off. I was raped and mugged. I slept in the streets. I am a woman. Hardly counts. If I were a bird, I'd give it and fly away with all the answer. A punk rock droll. Scatter and swift the chunky ashes, my progress as an organizer, as a woman. I'd get it in the small spaces where I try to listen. This act is simply and yet the failure rate is so monumental. Try these other handy forms of protest: topless tit waving, tear gassing babies, shaving your bush and sending it in the mail, taping your mouth shut.

It is about obstruction and raping (for little *women* tears):

They curb into the narrow

Disgust at the sight of   spoken in turn true doggerel: yet wispy in the way one carries out the trash:

like cheerleaders like little Barbie houses up for eviction   these are the pictures the pacifist takes and sends over the internet

scuttling refugees over the border with puns

I hate the public. The public operates the bus I used to catch on my way places. In the public there are homeless men who touch me with their large fingers and old women with their hot take-out food. Once there was a sign of a sexy blonde next to me every morning for a month. I became the public. This included all the times I pissed outside of a toilet, including on the steps of the church. There are also numerous encounters with public arousal, public masturbation at high speeds, public ejaculation, blow jobs, tit showing. I am the public. I hate the public when I grow this familiar with it. The only chance I have at finding some equilibrium is to arrive with some hoopla at a parade. Still to be announced. Part of my hatred translates as love I love the public. Like the Watts Towers. When given the opportunity to protest the public is always ready. The bodies accumulate and pushed together, as on the bus, there is always the chance to feel an erection up against the back of your thigh. This is part of the public I became.

For A.C.

Angela Jane Fountas

The Hydrologic Cycle

Clouds

She liked getting mugged. The hands on her purse, the rip. She let it swing from her wrist, weighted. Every mugger's heart skipped a beat. One came back, That fucking bird almost killed me.

She moves the cloud above him, her murderer. She wrings it dry. This takes all day. Push, squeeze. A few drops fall from the sky. Pigeon shit, he thinks, her wrung neck in his eyes.

Waves

She rubs herself with lard and dives in. The girl on the pier watches her red swimming cap against the gray waves that swell and break on the sand. Rain falls from the sky, disturbing the girl, not the swimmer.

My mother, the girl says, willing this to be.

When the swimmer emerges, the girl submerges, fully clothed. No! the swimmer feels in her throat, flashing back to the daughter she never had.

Not my mother, the girl bobs before giving in.

Silly fool, the swimmer says. We need each other.

Words

She butchers *meat* and buries *flower*, likes *cake* and *curt* but sucks back *hush*. She closes her ears to be. Her skin turns wax, candles sizzle and spit. She swaps *sky* for *sea*. Eats *breakfast* for lunch, breaks *bread* for ducks. Nobody knows *she* is *me*.

Love, she drowns, lying on top of each letter to hold it down.

Kelle Groom

Books & You

He said I was 44 Anna Kareninas, but I still had to go back home, unemployed, broke, I began to sell books I'd saved from the dumpster— *Springtime of the Liturgy* to Franklin,

New York, then*, Ideology: An Introduction* to Columbus, a *Reader's Greek-English Lexicon* to Waukesha, Wisconsin, another to Fort Lauderdale, *The New Testament World*

to Richmond, *Dangerous Liaisons* to Rockaway, *Deconstruction of the Visual Arts* to Fairfax, *Colonial Discourse* to Nashville, a *Concise Theological Dictionary* to a man in

Brecksville, Ohio who said he'd long been looking for this book. He said may God bless you, and I felt like he meant it. *Dialectic of Enlightenment* by Horkheimer to

Berkeley, *Pioneer Life* to Jacksonville. A little girl gets bit by a rattlesnake, and her brother (small) runs with her in his arms to a doctor far away who has one dose of snake

venom (needs two for a child), and she dies. *A Geneology of Pragmatism* to Upland, California, *Beguine Spirituality* to Seguin, Texas (signed), *Reading de Man Reading* to

Berlin, *A Grammatical Analysis of the New Testament* to another Upland in

Indiana, *Simians, Cyborgs, & Women* to Reseda, a *Theological Dictionary* to King's Park, New

York, *The Spivak Reader* to Upper Marlboro. The 19th book sold: *Culture and Imperialism*, Edward Said, to Middletown—"inability to conceive of any alternative—

made empire durable." Rousseau painting on cover: "The Representatives of the Foreign Powers Coming to Hail the Republic as a Token of Peace," 1907. I had never thought of

Jane Austin as an imperialist before. (Think of seeing a movie without him— sharp sadness & pull & love for his tender seeing of movies, everything— what is that pull? as

if my spirit-self makes a run for him but finds itself caught inside my body.) *The Black Atlantic* to Sandwich, *The Psychic Life of Power* to Culver·City. I dreamed a photograph

of the author last night in an Anne Sexton style, *Imaginary Bodies* to London with a beautiful blue painting, like clothing for a soul, produced at the Offenes Kulturhaus in

Linz, *The Heart Of the Matter* to Rockaway. The cloak of Elijah is in the Book of Kings, Pierre Teilhard de Chardin wrote his cloak essay in Jersey, in 1919, just after the war (the

cup appears to be closing over), *Critique & Power* to South San Francisco, *On Narrative* to the Berkeley School of Law, *Little Havana Blues* to Monument. I can't remember where I sent *Extreme-Occident*, (a little gauze coat with stars on it floating on a map of water), or *A Religious History of the American People* (over 300 people burned by Queen

Mary, see the Book of Martyrs, "made their sad way out to face the fires of Smithfield." *Pilgrim's Progress* written by Bunyan in jail. & the hymns of Issa Watts), or *Marxisim &*

the Philosophy of Language, "What are the procedures for uncovering, for seizing hold, so to speak, of inner speech?" Book #31: *In Spite of Plato* to the University of Verona,

(she weaves her bridal all day, unweaving at night, until he comes home, reminding me of the Beguine women, "a feminine space where women belong to themselves," also of

the Reformation, the Puritans believing a spiritual life is lived in the world, not in retreat from it. I thought for a while that Penelope was real, a real Queen, "maternity itself

can be a space"), *Looking Awry* to Lexington (Department of Geography), *Abjection, Melancholia, & Love* to Baltimore, *Selected Subaltern Studies* to Somerville, *An*

Introductory Guide to Post Structuralism to Petaluma, *Alternative to Speech* to Brooklyn, *Just As I Am*, by Robert Williams, the gay priest whose books are among these, whose

photo fell

out of one, who died, to Maidenhead, Berkshire, United Kingdom, *In Theory* to Berkeley, *More than Cool Reason* to West Lafayette. (I am a little lonely for the Waffle House at 3

a.m.), *An Anthology Of Essays from Dryden to Derrida* went I know not where, *Opening the Heart of Compassion* to Australia, *Jean de Florette* and *Manon of the Spring* to

Madison, movies I saw at the Enzian with Frank, at least in the time of Frank, Book #34: *Spiritual Exercises of St. Ignatius*—all I can see is the pyramid, a triangle of protection

for Jesus and Mary and Joseph, until the death of Herod, *Heidegger: A Critical Reader* to Irvine, the *Conquest of Happiness* to Harrisonburg (I send him little hints from

this book, hoping), a first edition of *Books & You*—mentions Johnson's *Lives of the Poets* (who was killed in the bar? All the endless photocopying I did of that book in the

library. Savage I think. I smelled the muck in front of Tangerine Avenue, where they dug for the new development, mountains of sinkhole muck that we stepped in, carefully,

knowing it was quicksand. Madame Bovary taught me not to die for money, how I'd thought I'd live for education, then die in darkest thinking or go to Europe. But seeing

Emma, I saw myself buying an armload of clothes, a red wool dress and coat. Whitman on this—the animals have no mania for owning things.) When I had to get a temp job, it

became harder to keep track of the books—*Perma Red* went, "Her grandmother had told her there were places along the river where water waited to be heard," *Women in the Acts*

of the Apostles and *Holy Listening*, "Even these may forget, yet I will not forget you. See I have inscribed you on the palms of my hands" Isaiah 49:15-16. I remember when my

parents said the way I drew the number 2 was beautiful. This was when I was still young enough to get a grade for handwriting in school, *Poetic Closure, The Secret Gospel,*

Clement of Alexandria, Medicine as Ministry—the myth of Tithonus, so handsome and loved by the goddess of the dawn who forgot to ask Zeus to give him eternal youth along

with immortality, and T became so old he folded up like a cricket in a basket; in pity, she turned him into one, a comforting noise in the summer night, "the suffering person to

whom I minister is the one sent to minister to me." What did I forget to ask for? The healing pool at Bethesda, *Jung, Synchronicity, & Human Destiny*, my brother called, said

"You go rock this world." He said, "I loved you all these years, I didn't know how to talk to you," *Zen Macrobiotics* (take a small spoonful of gomasio to neutralize your blood, stop eating honey, chocolate for a while), *Practicing Macrobiotics, Operating Instructions, Window of Vulnerability*, when the names of the martyrs are remembered in

church, they say, "Presente." He asked me to look for poetry/songs translated by Mark Strand ("Souvenir of the Ancient World"), I sold *Of Being Numerous, Out of Silence,* he

draws a bookstore for me on the edge of the sea, boats in the distance, I am so happy to have a place to live under the blue sky. After that I only sold what I could not say.

Kass Fleisher

Odyssey

3. superkalifragilistic

Hal, you open the fucking pod bay door or I'll kick your motherfucking blue-chip cocksucking silicon UIUC ass.

2. reconceptualization

The things she would give serious money not to think about anymore: (a) In October this place get kazillions of these goddamn ladybugs in town, ladybugs that aren't ladybugs at all but rather some Asian beetle brought in to eat pests in the field—(b) Gravity has yanked her ass down, so that when she stands in front of a mirror with her legs slightly apart, it looks as if she has finally grown some balls. (c) In walking on the trail, which used to be a railroad bed, she has to swat the damn—from her—

1. disestablishmentarian

They have been moved. Again. By the skin of their teeth, they belong now to the mass luxury class. They get flu shots annually. The possibility of a trailer park upon retirement—should there ever be a retirement—looms large in a not-so-distant-anymore future. I'll never live in a trailer, he says. What's wrong with a trailer, she says. My relatives lived in trailers—they did fine. We're not living in a fucking trailer, he says. Then too, there's the equation for a falling object – $v = gt$ with which you can measure the velocity of said falling object by multiplying the acceleration of gravity (32 feet per second squared, or 9.8 m/s^2) by the amount of time that's passed since its release. But you would only know, she says, the velocity in that split second. The velocity in the split second prior, and the velocity in the split second after, will be different. Yes, he says. So? So what is the point of measuring something that has already changed by the time we complete the calculation? To really know the precise velocity at a precise moment we'd have to be able to measure time to some infinite fraction. Can you measure, for instance, the precise moment in which you fell in love with me? Can you measure the precise moment, two hours later, when you fell out of love with me? And the moment perhaps two hours after that, when you fell back in? Can you measure the precise amount of time it's taking for these words to fall from my lips? For the words to tumble into your ear? Are we really as capable of these measurements as we think we are? As we desire to be? You there, me here, some immeasurable distance from one another? You dropping, in an airplane, forced by jet propulsion, through the air? Accompanied by resistance, by friction, by static, by misapprehension?

3. Hal? Open the pod bay door, Hal.

2. The things she would give

1.
again

Alexandra van de Kamp

My Breasts

They are the first to be touched by what's up ahead: clouds gather in the distance and beneath my shirt, each breast eagerly takes on the grainy gray of an old French film. Wherever I go, they go. They steer me forward, or each decision I make steers them. There is a causal relationship here, but I don't know where it begins and ends. Sitting by my bed one night, my father told me his version of a lullaby: that God is the one cause without a cause, and, thus, the supreme mover of the universe. I pictured a well-intentioned star blinking forlornly in an empty dark. None of us are gods. We adhere to wherever we are: the dirt paths and sooty boulevards. We feel the trees glue themselves into our scenes. You say a few words and they cling like damp leaves to my waiting skin. When I cry, I am never alone. The background intrudes, and I cry with windows, with pencils, with the blue umbrellas of the outdoor café at the Ritz Carlton, photographed in the postcard taped to my wall. My breasts are always near. They purr in a cool breeze, they know my fatigue. I remember our honeymoon and how you touched me through my white, see-through chemise. I know, we must not talk of such things (the world is full of a filthy breeze). *The body is a poem* you said that night you touched my breasts. And they knew, they knew before me, how short-lived such clarity is.

The Roof

is speaking today. Someone is up there, thumping and thumping away. My ceiling shivers. "Mr. Storm" my two-year-old niece says when she wants to name the rain. Outside, the day moulds itself into a silver screen—grays and blacks are coalescing, projecting bright curves and solid masses onto the sky beyond the trees. I feel photographed by someone I cannot see. What is a roof but a hat of tar or stone, a heaviness we wear above us, the upper edge of a frame we are always caught within. Our lives measured out in spoonfuls of clouds and shame, our feet stuck in the wet-paint of the now. That's why I love certain kinds of films, how the camera can pause and hover, like Goddard's zoomed-in-on coffee cup, the black inky cosmos swirling within, the clink of the spoon against the rim. I want to collect crisply cut scenes. And, at times, we move so languorously through our rooms ("a spot of tea for you" Mr. Fatigue?), but they are frames all the same nudging some plot forward. Who's watching my movie? My afternoon despair in which I watch the sun redden and singe the charcoal trees without knowing another new thing. I feel beneath a design larger than me, I feel beneath a sentence I cannot read. They are fixing the roof. Above me, it mutters and quakes. So, Mr. Roof, I ask, "What is it today?" I want an answer, I want a name, but instead it shakes and shakes.

Jon Davis

Accident

Andre Breton thought what thought thought could lead us into the glittering kingdom of the real. If we paid attention. If we let it happen. If we stopped impish reason, with its calculators and moral imperatives. If we let the cantilevered mushrooms collude with the vapid Chernobyls of our celebrated ancestry, the real would limp, shyly and remorsefully, from behind the curtain, speaking with her actual, though unamplified, voice. Andre Breton, whose wife's hair was a brush fire, whose thought was summer lightning, whose etc was an otter in the mouth of an etc. And the actual waiting for a cue. And the actual like a mouse among the table crackers.

And the cause of the accident was the woman's birth, her first steps on this wobbly planet. Her first grade teacher scolding her so that she withdrew from the math problems, the blurred numbers scattering like centipedes across the paper, and later she became a writer of advertising, and therefore, after college, moved to Manhattan, bought a Lexus, and, when the past deadline copy was finished, drove (the double yellow lines turning to centipedes in the just-before-sleep dream) off the road and through the newspaper stands lined alongside. The newspapers scattered, the weeklies and dailies, and the police report blamed her sleeping, but *she* knew, *she* knew—how each step, each decision, how each thought that thought thought had led her here, rain falling steadily on her shaking body, neck and back aching, hair tangled and soggy, the algebra turning into insects, the words glowing in their particularities, their unswerving allegiances, their habitats in their sentences, in their paragraphs. She knew, in the glare of the headlights, in the flash of red and blue, in the 3 a.m bustle, in the grind and roar, in the honk and clatter, in the streaming and gloaming and neverending of the gods' strange arrangements, she knew and, like Andre Breton, was delighted because she could not say she knew.

Maurice Kilwein Guevara

The Other Word for Thesaurus

Is treasure. Or *tesoro*. For *tesoro* I mean the toddler who is in a body cast because otherwise his spine may become permanently deformed. I don't believe in God. Look at the bones of his shoulders. He is opening presents on his third birthday and says thank you but wishes the little book were a train named Thomas. For Thomas is another way to say César Vallejo. I'll talk now only if I can turn away. Say this in Quechua or Arabic. There is a dead man or teenaged girl in the mountains witnessed by roads. There is infinity in the skull small enough for beaks to enter. In the reflected stars we each touch the letters hidden there.

Karen Holman

Hagiography

I was minding my own business working on my illuminated manuscript transliterating the song of the goldfinch, also known as the wild canary. I could see one perched on the feeder filled with thistles and thorns. Goldfinches symbolize gratitude for the Passion of Christ, his crown of thorns.

I took some liberties. I meticulously painted the breast and back of the goldfinch with gold leaf although its feathers are really yellow, the color of the discipline of hagiography. I painted its black mask, wings and fearless eye with lacquer. In my *Book of Hours,* John the Baptist has a crown of finches pulling his severed head by its dreadlocks straight into—an elevator's climbing trajectory—a heaven not visible to the naked eye. Heaven requires the raiment of a radio telescope, receptors stretching from here to a remote there to see if only in the mind's eye.

In my illustrations God is blue, plays a flute and is as entangled with Mary Magdalene as the flowering, twining vines in my illuminations. In my manuscript the sick heal themselves with their own magic spittle. For this, Christ is all gratitude. At the right hand of God a wild canary perches. On the left hand, too.

Brian Johnson

Self-Portrait (Ontological)

"I am" is a unit. It practices a few set formations. "I am going to bed" is a famous one. Also, "I am unhappy." "I am wasting my life" is now an old tune. For the sake of appearances, the "I am" unit assumes a false unity; the "I am" that scratches its pubic hair and swears, "I am in love with nothing," is not the same one that says, "I am truly blessed." The "I am" that shakes hands is always fighting the one that recoils, snakelike, at the slightest touch. The one that shares books is also the one that steals wives. The "I am" unit is held together by force, an unstable combination of willpower and magic: the world's strongest man relying on sleight-of-hand tricks. Breakdowns are frequent, but the underlying state of disrepair is patched and rigged and painted with amazing skill, so a sense of order prevails in the immediate circle of the "I am," allowing it to move and talk as professionals do. The desire of "I am" to be highly visible—to declare its name, race, and calling—overwhelms the wish to be invisible. Left to its own devices, "I am" would be anonymous and faceless, if not plural, a fact evidenced by authors who conceal themselves with multiple pen names and multiple styles. It is only when silence descends on the "I am," and it is reduced to more primitive gestures, that the world sees its poverty. As capable as the "I am" is of presenting itself, it is incapable of seeing itself without clothes, and without the declarations—"I am a writer," "I am from the Midwest," "I am married," "I am a Virgo"—that give drama to life. Only God has the strength to say, "I am that I am," for He alone can live without purpose, pleased with the vacuum He created.

David Lazar

Goodness Knows

Radical is latin for root, and each morning I pull myself out of bed and root for my better side to stay buried. When I was a boy, Mrs. Hall, from down the hall, would pull her Johnny up the stairs and say why couldn't he be like me, "always the straight and narrow." Mother closed the door behind me so father's strange song stayed inside.

When I was with the Brothers, I longed to be a single taper, the first vesper in the dark mornings. Brother Anthony's voice would caress mine during the sanctus, sliding vowels under my deepest piety.

Now I run some rum, and sometimes a sip or two will give me a vision of a worldly world with the trappings of paradise, which I've always thought was a quiet room painted blue with a hint of violet towards the door that seemed to know you—a door that opens silently, when you want it to, and maybe a window view gives an occasional glimpse of St. Bonnie or St. Clyde sitting in commerce with Bernadette or the Holy Ghost, though goodness knows you wouldn't see him, three sheets to the wind of God.

Goodness knows what led me to pull my heart out like a weed. The straight and narrow is buried somewhere inside me, parallel to my heart, in the shape of a tiny casket.

Michael Meyerhofer

If They Believed What They Told Us

we would know our greatest threat is not some errant warhead punted from the ocean, not a suitcase full of plutonium falling into the wrong hands (which is any hand but ours), not even a germ hacked free of the Amazon by capitalist loggers then blamed on San Francisco homosexuals, but instead, the primordial glow of the new mother openly nursing on a bench in Lantern Park, tipping herself like a pagan chalice into a mouth that never says thank you.

If she believed what her leaders say, she would know—this freckled mother with hair like solar prominence—that God is not inside her and all around her like the first Christians thought, but beyond, like an angry bearded whale who transcends all matter but his own. Or else God is the prototypical American who hath granted unto her alabaster skin and a mind like empty Tupperware, a dolly-heart kept fresh under tight folds of Glad Wrap. But she does not believe. Her child coughs, nestled within folds of chartreused wool.

Tonight, a million husbands will follow the *New York Times* best-seller list toward neo-messiahs who grin like Hannibal on blood-spangled paper jackets, toward Lady Justice brandishing what we thought was a John Wayne cavalry saber, but has since become a scimitar—so bright with day's decline that even mothers forget the mastectomy scars. Please remember: under the blindfold, those eyes are made of stone. And if the sunburnt priests of Babel could see us now, even they would turn away, shaking their unwashed heads.

Michael Koshkin

1

I search *mobile destruction*. I search it in quotes. I search *ending method*. I am coming apart. The light makes me sick. It is constant.

My eyes are planets. They are filled with gasses. And many morons revolve around them. That is—moons.

2

My friend's dad, when we were kids, woke up one day and saw darkness in the bottom left corner of his eye. At breakfast he poured salt into his coffee and we just watched silently. By noon he was knocking over books and fine paper weights in his office. That evening what looked like a hood draped over his left eye.

The following morning a large blue vein was bulging over his eyebrow. My friend's mother told him to relax. That his vision would come back shortly.

After seeing a doctor, he was rushed to a hospital in Houston where they sliced open a layer of his retina and stuck a needle behind it, injecting what was said to be a gas of some sort. He laid face down in a hospital for three weeks and waited for the gas to leak out.

3

I copy down a list of volatile chemicals and tack it to my fridge. I comb the pawn shops for tools. Looking for a socket set, but I keep finding scratch awls. Elton John plays on secondhand stereos everywhere. He is singing for me. He wants me to win. I see things I used to own. Or maybe I imagine that. Everything looks so familiar. Everything is in plastic cases.

I don't sleep. Again, I look to the internet. Copy down lists of theories on ending the world. Each theory with its ingredients and plausibility. I copy down the ones that begin with the destruction of biological creatures. I go see a shrink. It doesn't work.

I am told to find a sanctuary. To eat black lentil soup and replace liquor with pot. I am told these things will cure me. I am told to stop with the research.

4

Swallowed up by a black hole is not so likely. Less likely than being melted by the sun or enormous fires caused by an assortment of Buick-sized meteors. The others all blur together. Something about grey matter. The exhaled breaths of polar bears that have become plagued by seals igniting in frozen desserts. Or maybe that's wrong.

I crouch in the tub. Watch the neighbor's light flick off. Consider the likeliness of them watching me through the bathroom window—pecking their beaks on the glass. Everyone buzzing. My skin is beginning to shed. Or could it molt? Or are they the same thing? I go back to the ending methods.

5

A silhouette of flying eyeballs. Maybe not flying. But eyeballs with wings. Smudges on my glasses. Graves are perfect geometric shapes. In the forest somewhere. People—Forest people. They hum.

I feel nauseous. I don't have time to dry off. I lay on the carpet with sweatpants wrapped over my face. All around me a buzzing.

Christine Gelineau

Scat

Coyote leaves its scat like a phone number in a public restroom. Doberman is salivating to answer the call. Sure, he's heard the Trickster stories but what can you tell a Doberman? He's on a quest, the quest, and the scent is fine as he gambols through the dappled forest, dreaming his delights. Who is there really to blame when the pack jumps him just for sport? Who's to say he won't always treasure his scars, the lackadaisical tilt to his torn ear, the memory of sweet shriek and snarl among the trees?

Liana Scalettar

Smallpox Hospital Nocturnes

I. Blackwell's Island, 18--

Sally says, what you must do is to begin very slowly to open your eyes upon your new home. What you must do is to begin very slowly to crochet with the thinnest pearliest thread countless rosettes, heaps and heaps of them, and when you have amassed some fine quantity—*a hundred?*—a fine quantity of them, then you may begin to string them together, turning them into the hems and necks of shirts and smocks and things. *But*—. Sally says, I will write to you as you are the dearest of all my nieces but of course visiting is prohibited. Of course they say Blackwell's Island is studded, crammed full of ghosts like figs in a fig pudding. *Like figs*—. In a fig pudding. They say. They say you will begin to forget your life outside, how you loved the snow on Madison Square, how you loved the trolley cars' scarlet carapaces, how you loved green melon sherbet in a little silver dish, how you loved Mr. Matt Marshing who is I will tell you desolated by your removal. Sally says, my dear, look a little livelier; surely you can't have already begun such an unseemly fading?

Starshot, like gun or lead or any shot, reaches us through tiny blackened window panes designed it seems to prevent us from remembering the city. We wander around in muslin gowns, of which the laces trail flaggingly, and we concentrate on doctors' proceedings. In an unused corner, string flowers accrue. Everyone, it seems, has a Sally. Everyone has a Matt Marshing. Dear, says an older lady, don't slump over like a ruined soufflé. Aerate—that's the great thing—aerate those poxy pink lungs.

II. Roosevelt Island, 19--

⚙ Sentence 5

In the old hospital, in the old stone heap, in the tower, in the second floor, where I wait in a sheet and some swanfeather winglings, where I stand stock still like a statue in the ouverture of the performance piece by the famous Irish director, for the fancy summer festival. It's night. O that this. Nightlong. Audience members will come one by one and see me: in this silver-painted room, in this straw pile mixed with pastel rags, in this niche where I stand and am angelic. And am demonic. And am braided into twenty silver-painted braids and am plated with a masque of silver paint and am standing. The room, 100 X 100 feet, emptied of iron bedstands, of aprons, of pinafores, of muslin, of ewers, of pewter basins, of bacilli, of viruses, of phlegm, of blood, of snot, of skin, of cells, of nucleii, of riboflavins, of men and women, of boys and girls.

III. Roosevelt Island Tramway, 20--

Because you didn't know of the hospital's existence, because you'd been to this sliver of land once as a small boy, because we discussed old stilted houses, Vinegar Hill, whiskey, ice, animal crackers, elephants, icing on the cake, the greenhouse effect, chalk and its slipperiness, flowers, marathons and the gold way words leave traces, I'm writing this nocturne about our traveling in the tram together to Roosevelt Island. It's a reverie. It will never happen. It has not happened. If it does happen, I will deny ever having wished it to happen and especially ever having written this little number. I omit here the cheap B-movie dialogue I never ever (ever!) expected to hear sounded in my own voice. I say nothing about my future hopes, my unborn children, your impossible eyelashes and the eyes they're over, or anything else. It also goes without saying, but I'm saying anyway, *you make fiction impossible.* So here we are swaying in the tram, at night.

The building is now known and has been known for some time as the Renwick Ruin.

Neil de la Flor

Joey and the Banshee

I

Banshee: In Gaelic folklore, a spirit of a woman who appears, wailing, to signal that somebody in the household is going to die.

1492: Christopher Columbus. Columbus, Ohio. The Buckeye State. Black-eyed peas. Bratwurst. In Toledo I met a man named Chris. He ran a Christmas shop stocked with Santas and snow. Summer Sale, the sign read. He sold me my first set of pinecones and a bunch of mistletoe.

Peace, he said, gently placing two dimes and a penny in my hand. *And come back again.*

II

Applesauce: If there's anything the almost dead will almost always eat, it's applesauce. Mott's brand works best, cinnamon or no cinnamon, it doesn't matter. It's not the taste, but the way it slides easily down the throat that makes them appreciate it, especially when the tongue stops working and the lips too.

III

Death is a frame containing a photograph or drawing of a child's profile, or of a moonlit stagecoach hunted by wolves in winter.

IV

It is insane, the running of the bulls, the trampling of the willing down cobblestone streets, streets once ruled by Romans who devised cities within walls built of stone.

I once knew a boy, an heir to Bacardi, his name was P. His family loved Cuba and liquor. Who was I to argue with his sex appeal, the way he shouldered so much sugarcane on his back. Finally, when the revolution called for cinco (5) words he hollered, *uno, dos, tres,*

cuatro, cinco!

V

You see, the Gaelic spirit, that wailing woman, she is a bull. She tramples down streets without direction.

Joey: One day I saw him standing in the middle of the street hailing a cab, like a wailing woman he was hollering, hands miss-thinging in the air, *Taxi! Taxi!* It seemed like the whole world stopped for him—taxi, pedestrian, me—and we held our collective breath as he turned around to see who was watching him and who was not, then gave us the finger.

Get in, Joey said. *I don't have all night.*

James Fowler

All Bars Have Ghosts

Everytime a barfly cries into a drink, a drunk yells at a waiter, someone throws a drink in someone else's face, a little bit of them leaks out. The glowing particles gather together in the dark near the ceiling. The older the bar, the stronger the ghost. My grandfather used to come to this bar, and his grandfather and grandmother first met here. This ghost is family. It just talked me into having another whiskey, when I should be getting home to my empty apartment, where I can listen to my ex-girlfriends yell at me about the rent money, where I can hear them say that I'm worthless, that my family has always been worthless.

Jay Snodgrass

My Ghost Made an Art Movie

1.1

My ghost made an art movie in which there was language and therefore god. She was over beside the window with her camera. It was her *eye*. I was impressed with the heft of her glow. Staunch and reverent. I'm growing a plant in my mind. It's mint in a pot on the back porch. If it dries out and dies because I forgot to water it no big loss. I'll think of something else. Plant wilts in B&W.

1.2

My ghost made an art movie in which I served drinks at a party. No one came and I was sad, hence the ghost. The drinks were mojitos with fresh mint from my mind. They say Castro has a ghost he serves drinks to also. Which must be why he so often weeps.

19.1

My ghost is a little girl. Which would explain all the animals like stuffed toys. The only thing is they really are animals whose insides have been removed and replaced with cotton stuffing. They lay around with tufts of white cotton poking out, turning red. Clotting and getting stuck to the couch. My ghost has a pony on a tether. She hauls it back and forth across the screen. When I look, the horse is alive. It's eyes, close up, swivel in terror.

19.2

It is not insignificant that my ghost has a crowd of film critics in a pen. They are all howling and nude. Mostly older white men in flab and gray hair. This grizzled exposure shows just how far my ghost will go for a favorable review. The best thing I can hope for is to come away with my sanity. The camera follows past the men as they yell and cheer or cry and fall to the ground. The camera zooms in on me. I am standing in the middle of this crowd. I look up, surprised to be there when a faceless inspector takes me by the arm and leads me in to the dark of screen.

Siobhán Scarry

Jubilate: Burden, Kansas

For grain dust is fine and slips through the fingers.

For grain becomes bread that we break in your memory.

For grain is transported by ships and trains and long flat boats.

For grain is stored in buildings that rise up from flat land.

For grain elevators are strangely the poetry of the American sky.

For they are built in various shapes according to landscape and function.

For the buildings are pure in their geometry.

For the circle is unity.

For the triangle is the trinity.

For square and rectangle are pleasing in their shapes.

For the hexagon is the geometry of the bee.

For bees, in their building of honeycombs, gave rise to the schematics of
interlocking grain bins.

For hexagonal bin design does not waste space—there is no need for the
strangely shaped interstitial bins.

For the longest elevator in the world uses hexagonal bin design—praise the
grain elevator in Hutchinson, Kansas.

For elevators are made of many materials.

For we are woken to life by knowing decay.

For wood is decay.

For tile decays.

For steel bins do not insulate the grain.

For vermin get inside the bins and gorge themselves on the fine dust of
harvest.

For life is decay.

For the abandoned silos are in decay.

For there is dust in our lungs.

For all creatures will come to dust.

For it is true—and I have seen it—that grain dust explodes.

For spontaneous combustion is proof of a Presence—Remember the thirty-three men who died at the Husted Mill in 1913.

For dust clings to elevators, even those converted to hotels and artists' lofts.

For firstly, the grain is moved upward in the elevator by small buckets on conveyor belts.

For secondly, the grain is moved to the distributing floor, where it is weighed and chalkboards mark the weight and grade and destination.

For thirdly, the grain is moved along conveyor belts and lowered into the bins through small holes that the men try not to fall through.

For fourthly, the grain is stored for months or years or else it is moved quickly through chutes onto boats or railcars waiting below.

For the storage and transport of grain is a wholesome enterprise.

For it is pleasing to feel the slip of grain between the fingers and hear it crunch underneath boots on the cement workfloor—Be gracious to the elevator in Burden, Kansas.

For each handful of grain comes from a field of growing things—Be gracious to the cribbed wooden elevator in Attica, Kansas.

For fields from above are geometrically pleasing—Save the condemned silos of Minnesota.

For there is Presence in the swish and movement of grain particles colliding in the chutes.

For the storing of grain in large bins is the desire for tomorrow—Bless the peeling letters of C and T and A on the silo in Lake City, South Dakota.

For the Dakotas are desolate and need their landmarks.

For those states have been spared with silos spaced evenly along the railroad, every fifteen miles.

For people in Kansas are more needy—Bless the four-mile intervals.

For there is something to be said for the even spacing of certain kinds of
    structures.

For it is important to love the spaces in between—Remember the insterstitial
    bins with shapes that accommodate.

For flat-bottomed bins are useless for unloading but have pleasing shapes.

For flat land must have shapes that rise up in praise. Bless Aldo Rossi.

For silos desire upward motion.

For the workfloor is the ground level—Praise the wood elevator of Chokio,
    Minnesota.

For the storage bins are the body of the building—Give us this day our
    daily bread.

For the distributing floor has many windows but workers keep their eyes on
    the floor to avoid falling through—Praise the buckling slats of the
    elevator in Lucas, Kansas.

For the headhouse sits on top of the building—Bless the small dusty
    windows of elevator headhouses.

For any structure so solid is a monument to the everlasting—A blessing on
    Danville, Kansas where the 18-bin silo dwarfs the church (bless its
    steeple and the lonely slatted window).

For structures this large have SPIRIT inside them.

For SPIRIT is fullness.

For SPIRIT is round in its shape.

For round structures have no end and converge with the sky in an
    understanding of infinity.

For it is most common for grain bins to be round.

For common shapes are pleasing to the gods.

For storage is proof of thinking of tomorrow.

For allow me to consider a single spark in Wichita, Kansas.

For every spark does not ignite.

For desire cannot be predicted.

For sparks are in every careless cigarette lit on the workfloor.

For sparks fly from the steel rails of nearby train tracks.

For fire is the particular fear of grain elevator workers.

For fire CONSUMES.

For CONSUME is a word that feeds on itself, desires more than itself.

For the word keeps circling in the mouth when you are done saying it.

For a spark with the desire to CONSUME felled the DeBruce grain elevator
    four miles southwest of Wichita, Kansas.

For due to management negligence, on June 8th, 1998, a concentrator roller
    bearing seized from no lubrication and locked the roller into a static
    position as the conveyor belt continued to roll over it.

For this is called the "razor stop" effect—Imagine machinery at 260 degrees
    Celsius.

For these are the conditions that join fire with dust.

For seven men died that day for America's bread—Rest the souls of Jose
    Luis Duarte (41 years), Howard Goin (64 years), Lanny Owen
    (43 years), Victor Manuel Castaneda (26 years), Raymundo Diaz-
    Vela (23 years), Jose Prajedes Ortiz (24 years), and Noel Najera
    (25 years).

For even in its hell-bent desire, the spark could not reach all the bins.

For steel is strength.

For concrete is strength.

For the metal clasps on the lunch boxes are strength.

For the flat land is filled with structures that are still standing.

For when traveling in certain states, one elevator passes from view just as
    another appears on the horizon.

For elevators carry the eye upward to sky.

For elevators reach.

Richard Gwyn

Ancestor Worship

No one knew where the king was. He had slipped away from the breakfast room, speaking obscenities. He had not read his newspaper. He had not eaten his two eggs, boiled for precisely two minutes, nor had he finished his hot chocolate. The chancellor was aggrieved: he had, as usual, important issues to bring to the king's attention, issues that could not be postponed. Servants were sent to find the king. The searched the palace and the cellars below the palace. They searched the stables. They looked up trees and peered down wells. The king was not to be found. The queen was reported to be distraught. As the day progressed it became increasingly difficult to keep the news of the King's disappearance within the palace walls. Walls have ears. People talk. In the city, the price of gold began to plummet. But in the evening, the king reappeared, and took his customary place at the head of the dinner table. He was dressed entirely in leaves. Damp soil clung to his face and the royal beard was matted with burrs and spiders' eggs. His hair was crawling with lice and dung-beetles. Everyone was staring at him. *What's the matter with you all?* He growled, reaching for a haunch of meat. *Never felt the need to spend the day beneath the earth?*

Julia Story

When I Was There

Two lady cops offered me a job sorting road kill. "Sort it how?" I asked, squinting into their headlights. "We're not really sure," they said, "there's the bags down there." One coughed into a hanky. They pointed down the hill to the bags. Night was coming on. The bags were large and very still. Fortunately, I had worn my bandana. I walked down to the sigh of cops finally driving away.

The first thing I pulled out of the bags was a type of dog. It didn't smell like anything except a smell I describe today as "night." A mysterious substance hardened its fur. One eye was normal and one twisted to glance at me, as if I had offended it. Its legs were mangled but I straightened them as best I could and set the dog down. It leaned. Its color is best described when I tell the story today as "dog brown." I realized what I had just done and put my hands over my ears, because something told me that a terrible sound was coming. Nothing. The muffin-colored hills sloped toward us; the darkening gloves of the trees. The dog began to move. First it limped as though learning to walk, and then like it had known all along but had been taught by something other than a dog. It jerked and tottered and its neck creaked around and its eyes told me that it didn't want this life. I pulled him out because it was my new job, and then all of the bags emptied themselves and many staggering moles and crusty possums filled the valley, and even one dead man stood up and watched it all through eyes that were part of a sort of necklace that hangs in the sky, eyes that used to close when things like this happened—all those times when I was somewhere else feeling lost.

⚙ Sentence 5

Monique van den Berg

Red Hysteria

My nickname for my period is Karl Marx. I think it demands that my femininity be taken seriously, especially in political circles.

One thing I never understood, when I was in grade school, was why we hated the communists. Reagan was president then; we were learning history. So much was dependent on the evils of communism, but nobody could explain it specifically. In Catholic school, explanations were frowned upon.

Every twenty-six or twenty-seven days Karl Marx comes over, and I ask him about it. "Karl," I say, pouring him a brandy, "Why do capitalists hate communists?" He pats my arm and calls me a clever girl. He stays for a week, eats everything in my refrigerator, drinks all my top-shelf liquor, but never answers the question. I suspect he doesn't take me seriously.

The Dead Bird

There is no such thing as a dead bird.

This was joyous news to the girl, whose canary had died three years before. "Mother!" she shouted. "There's no such thing as a dead bird!"

Out of her pockets the mother drew her two cupped hands. She opened them and out fluttered the yellow bird.

"I thought you'd never figure it out," the mother said.

Mark Cunningham

Starling

I once knew a guy named Starling, but I don't know if he could speak Latin and Greek like the one Pliny the Elder heard. I bet my Starling was more like Ben Jonson's Shakespeare: he knew little Latin and less Greek. Well, I bet he knew "Ixnay." I know Roman numbers, I even know that the original for "four" wasn't IV but IIII, but I don't want to get involved with anything over XCLXVIII. Speaking of Shakespeare, I once did Mark Antony as Yogi Bear: "I have come not to bury Caesar but to look inside his pic-anic basket." Just like in Shakespeare, it was a riot. I *have* read Zukofsky's translation of Catullus, in which the English sounds like the Latin and keeps the meaning; academics say that can't be done, so they ignore it. Enlightenment and idiocy are speechless when truly realized. Catullus is the sparrow. I murmur, murmur, murmur.

Eskimo Curlew

The man who owns the video store I go to is named Mark. When I go to the Toyota dealer, Mark writes up my service ticket. Mark is one of the few people from grad school I still meet around town. When I moved from one side of town to the other, the first person I met was Mark. Basho writes

Fall—
my neighbor,
how does he live?

For over a week, I haven't seen the 80-year-old woman who lives by herself next door. Lights go on and off, but that could be her great-niece checking an empty house. Sometimes at night a shadow dims the bedroom curtain: a branch shadow or my own eyes shifting? I don't want to know what my neighbor does. I don't care if she watches *Court TV* and has four dead-bolts on every door or if she solves the *New York Times* crossword puzzle while recalling her days in the physics lab. But I want her there. I want some area that's not had its life pinned down, I want some openness. Now and then, I see clouds blow over the corner of her roof and I remember the gradeschool feeling that the clouds are still and the earth is moving. Then I remember it's not. Then I remember it is.

Christopher Buckley

Infinity

Everything is formless where the waves break into the sky, rain and the unremarkable unraveling of the sea. And still the air in shambles. Any oncologist knows you are four times more likely to contract cancer living in L.A. The elementary machinery of salt gave us early warnings up the coast as I J-Waxed the pits from the chrome on my '59 Bel Air. No one was praying for the ocean then.

The taxonomy of pathos dissipates in no time over drinks, the poor reproving nothing, come quarterly dividends. The drug conglomerates won't even look at ALS; not enough of us die annually to make it profitable. The President is going to Mars.

Wind blows its madness and white caps off shore. Around the fast food dumpsters, gulls implement late capitalism—I got mine, how'd you make out? Ah, the white, Chamber-of-Commerce ranchitas of the clouds. Come on—the soul looks out on dust.

Yes, I'm not doing anything for lunch. I'm no longer even a Romantic, and know enough to mistrust the sweetness of the world. A few years into my last loneliness, my surviving vices are marginal at worst. The stars, grey as ever, are redundant from here. They burn their way into the past, though we discovered that only recently. Sure, the waves are tipped with light—stars washing away in the tide.

I came to touch the sea—to feel its afterthoughts evaporate from my fingers... Infinity has always driven me up a wall. The white dinner plate of the moon, the invisible veil of star dust drifting down—it's all beyond us. And I can no more start a new life than that dog who streaked out like a comet from the wide empty fields along Hwy. 41 in front of my silver rent-a-car. The white stars of his teeth, the dull sticks of the belly and leg blasting away to the dark hovering forever there at the roadside's edge—its poor bright blood sinking back to salt, to water, to a spume of atoms far from any sea we know.

My 25th Guggenheim Application

I'm nothing, if not persistent. I still want to save the whales, and baby seals, even the battery chickens. America never got a good 5¢ cigar. And I never lived in NYC, though I ate lunch there a time or two. I know New Formalists in high places, but can't escape the ranks of the politically expendable, the plain ignorable. "We don't do business with people we don't do business with." I needed Burt Lancaster to write for me from Atlantic City.

My books come back still shrink-wrapped, thrown through the hopeless window. I command enough romance languages to sweet talk my way through a menu at restaurants where I have to put it on the VISA card, the "Never-Never," as the Brits have it. With the passing of time, and money into the appropriate hands, some of my friends have even turned into Republicans, joined the Knights of Columbus, and they won't share the secret handshake. Some drive pick-up trucks that cost as much as Cadillacs—some drive pick-ups that *are* Cadillacs. They are no help to me or anyone. In this they resemble my relatives.

I don't deserve a MacArthur; I'm not a genius—I don't know the right people. I'm not going to The Club, not lifting a Manhattan and crustless sandwich off a silver tray. And despite poetry's diminishing returns, I continue to be confused with the Christopher Buckley from Yale, the one who writes snappy bits for *Esquire* and *TV Guide*, the guy with the Smoking movie, with the famous father just to the right of Hammurabi. I was called to be on the TODAY SHOW to chat about my speech writing for George

Bush the First—I declined, and they figured I was just trying to leverage a higher fee—it's business. I could have shown up and given the network pundits premature ventricular contractions with my views on Late Capitalism, but the other Buckley is tall and blond, has a blue blazer and entourage, and I'd have seen a check for my expenses about the time Haiti freezes over—but given Global Warming, perhaps I should have given it a shot.... Political currency. That's what I need. "It Takes Money to Make Money"—inscribed over the gate as they turned for a last look at Eden.

I've got a day job, have stood with my hand raised and not lost my place in line. When the phone doesn't ring, it's Oprah, living only a few streets over from where I grew up in Montecito. As for career fulfillment, I remember Lee Trevino BBQd by a bolt of lightning while out there on the job—how hard or long he'd worked had nothing to do with it. He said the next time the weather went south, he'd hold up a 1-iron as even God can't hit a 1-iron. Lee and I share some views on administrators, and like him, I've worked regular hours and tried to keep my head down, I've paid attention to the risk/reward ratio, though he's lined up a few more endorsements than I have.

By the time I was invited to read at the Dodge Festival in New Jersey, Bill Moyers was long gone—another missed opportunity for TV fame and fortune. And the reading wasn't in the big main tent. My pal Len and I were two hundred yards south, off in the woods, a left turn past the port-o-potties, in the clearing with the splintery folding chairs. But on the ride back to the hotel, I shared a van with Yehuda Amichai, who was happy to talk with me though he knew me from no one. His poems risked everything in front of God, and in their modesty, their rough grace and gravity, he had the poverty of our bones almost glowing. He'd been through war, and love,

Sentence 5

worn the gloves of the dead, and still he had a little hope to share. He could tell I knew his work, and he had a smile for me despite the unopened *Selected* I asked him to sign. The only application he had pending was for more time to write and walk among the garden. He didn't beg.

Sandy McIntosh

Insignificant Meetings with Remarkable Men

"The un-readiness is all." —attr. G. I. Gurdjieff

1. My father knew General Eisenhower. I was four or five. He took me to meet the ex-president during half-time at a Colgate vs. Army football game. "How are you, my boy?" Eisenhower asked, patting my head. "I have to wee-wee," I supposedly answered. He bent down and supposedly confided, "I do, too."

2. On Fifth Avenue, on the way to the "Merry Mailman" kiddies television program, waiting to cross the street with my father, I pulled the gun out of a big cop's holster. The cop whipped around while my father stood back. "Gimme that, you little bastard!" I was upset that the cop had shouted, and so probably cried.

3. The Great Someone-Or-Other (a once-famous magician reduced to performing at children's parties) tried to amaze us with a trick in which you drop shredded newspaper into a cake pan, cover it, say the magic words and a real cake appears. I was smarter, though. I had my own magic kit. I rushed to the stage and unmasked the cake pan's false bottom. I received no applause, and the magician looked sad.

4. The principal of my progressive school had a persistent fascination with Alain, a classmate from Haiti. "It's the chicken guts," Alain told me. "Everyone in my family tells the future by chicken guts." According to Alain, the principal would call him from his classes and they would

---

164 ○ Sentence 5

meet under the apple tree, where the principal would question Alain about the divination of the stars and the planets. Alain asserted: "He believes everything I tell him." Of course, I didn't. The principal was a stern disciplinarian and nobody's fool. But years later I heard he'd been fired, losing the school's money in inexplicable transactions. Reportedly, he pinned the blame on his personal oracle.

5. The summer before I was sent to military school my father introduced me to an older boy who attended there. Grown up, the boy is now a well-known real estate tycoon, owner of gambling casinos, and a famously angry star of his own TV show. At school, he was always nice to me, though he never laughed at my jokes.

6. Our military school chaplain was a war hero, credited with killing many men, though a priest. One afternoon, he caught me under the library with cigarettes. He ordered me to his office, reappearing in military uniform. I expected a tongue-lashing lecture. Instead, he marched me to the commandant's office, whining: "This boy! A member of my religious instruction class!" The commandant awarded me thirty punishment tours to be marched in dress uniform, a big M-1 rifle on my shoulder. I never respected the chaplain after that. He used to close his sermons with quaint New England expressions, such as "Keep your peckers up, boys." He'd seem bewildered when we'd laugh at him— gleefully taking his good wishes the wrong way.

7. At fourteen, the books of the English humorist, P.G. Wodehouse, entranced me. On a family trip to England after my father's death, I had hoped to meet the famous writer. But a publisher friend of the family told me that Wodehouse hadn't lived in England for years. In fact, he was living in America, only thirty minutes from my home. Back in the States, I looked up his address and wrote to him. He answered in one

line, "Sorry. I never knew your father."

8. I attended college in the Hamptons, home of many painters. The Abstract Expressionist, Willem de Kooning taught elementary painting. "It's lonely in the winters," de Kooning told me. "It was either teach with your friends or get drunk with them every night." Once, driving to his studio on an errand, I'd brought my girlfriend. De Kooning offered me Scotch. Then on the wagon, he insisted on watching me drink. When I'd finished, he chased my girlfriend around the studio. As soon as I could, I gathered her up, and we left, despite his offer to show us his latest paintings.

9. With Chiara, the ten-year-old daughter of a friend living in Venice, I crossed the bridge to Ezra Pound's home. Chiara and Pound played chess now and then. Pound and Olga Rudge met us at the door. Though supposedly in his silent period, Pound was full of conversation. "We play all the time. She always beats me," he told me. "But do you play?" I told him I didn't. Silent then, he turned and headed for the chess table. Olga Rudge made me a cup of Lapsang Souchong tea. "He loves his game," she told me. Crossing the bridge on the way home, I asked Chiara how it had gone. "Beat him, as usual," she answered.

10. A year later I returned to Venice. The last boat for Il Cemetario was leaving and I'd just had time to catch it. Pound had died, and was buried near the graves of other idols: Igor Stravinsky and Serge Diaghilev. I'd only begun to search for them when, behind me, a bell pealed. I turned and saw the great wooden doors of the cemetery closing. I escaped but had seen nothing I'd come to see.

11. As a student at Columbia, I was given plum assignments, escorting visiting writers around the campus. I met Jorge Luis Borges, the blind

aristocrat poet, at his subway stop and offered my help. His translator and aide, Norman Thomas di Giovanni answered for him: "Thanks, but we can find our own way. After all, I went to school here." Later, I was asked to help the famous poet and communist, Pablo Neruda, to the airport. "No need," his driver told me. "He'll take his limousine."

12. "One knew other poets when one was at university," W. H. Auden told us on a visit to our classroom. "But one would never expect to find them in such an odd thing as a Creative Writing class." Auden was wearing a blue terry cloth bathrobe and sipping a Martini. (I can't be sure of this.) He proceeded to denigrate all poetry except traditional meter as a means for teaching students. He offered to help us learn the classical forms. I don't know how many students returned for his next class. Being a modernist, I didn't go.

13. At the Cathedral of St. John the Divine, they were dedicating the Poet's Corner. Later, Robert Penn Warren stopped me in the street. He'd been a guest of honor at the ceremony, but now wanted directions to the subway. I did my best to be detailed and exact. After all, he was an old man and might get lost. I even offered to ride with him to his destination. When I'd finished he said: "No, I think I'll take a cab."

14. Jean Erdman, wife of Joseph Campbell, had produced a play by a friend of mine. At the reception held at their apartment, I ran into Campbell on the balcony, gazing at the twilight sky. What a wonderful chance; however, I'd read none of his books. "Nice evening," he observed with his familiar lisp. I agreed that it was, indeed, a nice evening. He turned and walked back inside.

15. Years after I'd been his student, I became a teaching colleague of the only poet on the English department faculty. We had been good friends,

but he'd betrayed me. "How many poets do you think *can be* on an English department faculty?" he asked after he'd blocked my tenure. I was angry, plotting revenge. Not till years later did I see a chance for it. My enemy had become deformed with Parkinson's, his arms festooned with bandages. "It's the drugs," he complained. "When I dream, I act out. Last night I punched my fist through the window." Now I felt nothing but pity—no pleasure at all.

16. I published a long poem about a writer I'd known in graduate school, a terrific manipulator. Thoroughly self-centered but brilliant, he often disparaged my projects publicly, claiming later that I shouldn't be surprised as I was "the competition." At a book fair, years later, where my new book was on display, I was staggered when he appeared in person, walking down the aisle. He had aged, but over the years had gained national fame and respect from readers and other writers. I was sitting behind the counter, watching him approach. Without noticing me, he examined my book cover in familiar head-tilted, birdlike posture. I was thrilled that he might buy my book! I imagined his surprise when he'd begin the poem and instantly recognize himself! He stared for a time at the book cover, but walked away without saying anything.

17. Trying on a leather jacket, I commented to the clerk that a few silver studs would make it look really cool. "The stud," replied the clerk, "is inside the jacket." As I admired myself in the mirror I noticed that I was taller, leaner, sexier—dangerous looking. What a revelation! This was the real me: a remarkable man! I imagined a new life of wild successes, overmastering men, seducing women. However, the jacket turned out to be too expensive, so I bought a different one.

—*for Denise Duhamel*

Edward Bartók-Baratta

The Submission

I'm an imbecile.

Wanting to send out poems, I begin by walking in the opposite direction.

The men in the park pass their unholy brown paper bag.

Each mentally calculates how long each of the others pulls on the upturned
bottle.

Only other liberal imbeciles like me expect wisdom from them.

Yet, they are wise to a thing or two. Their expectations do not exceed the
contents of the bag.

I wake to the clock, disgusting news. Having wet my hair, I drink tea.

I find clothes from last night where I had dropped them.

Suddenly I'm outside, wearing the same ideas, carrying in my hand the
submission.

I am not in a villa in the south of Italy.

I'm in a city, filthy because of the fourth week of a garbage strike.

If all of us stopped showering, we could come to realize that we are
animals.

I read the newspaper, how disgraceful we were yesterday, and are expected
to be tomorrow.

Writing in the margins, I am at work on the submission.

I'm not growing food, which involves turning the soil, inadvertently cutting
worms in half with my spade.

I'm not delivering a baby who may grow up to be a ruthless dictator, an
astronaut, or a ballerina.

Scribbling like thousands of other imbeciles, I'm obsessed with the thought
that I am unique and important.

Despite the idea of my bloated worth, the men in the park allow me into
their circle.

They stare at one another's shoes, the subdued enthusiasm taught to them by
other days like this one.

They maintain a tolerant silence while I read the submission.

Road Test

Can anybody tell me what a road is?

A road is a place where you put your eyeglasses, sir.

Respondent one, that's fine, last waking act before sleep.

Civil engineers are children who've never grown up: a road is a line shot like a dart through an enormous field so that later they can admire it from a helicopter in the sky.

Someone give that person a foil-wrapped kiss.

The Brooklyn Bridge is a short hair that fell from the sky where two giants were making love on a couch in 1923.

But is the turtle courageous, the moon pulling her across?

Which says nothing about the punk rocker who safety-pins a chicken's beak to his leather,

or the eggs that hatch, and one day will have to cross back.

The crow eats a fishhead, accustomed to you at sixty-five miles an hour.

The bird's awkward philosophy and the stitches that connect us;

the modern soul and the roadkill.

Ed Orr

Pascal Interrupts

Only the painter takes himself out of the picture. Courbet understood when he painted over himself to expose a nude with a parrot. The parrot, however, must have been of two minds as it recalled what little it could of penetrating and being penetrated—abstract as all intercourse, yet concrete as well, and coarse, a thing both with and without feathers, given to flights of fact and fancy as music, Mozart, who, like the painter and the parrot, must have had other things in mind as he committed notes to paper, filling in between and on the lines, like blackbirds on a fence or telephone wires, blackberries on a bush, only more purposeful, more conscious of some desired end.

"The notion that mechanical motion is hostile to reason or the spirit, because it cannot think or love erratically as men do, is one of those absurdities that render the talking world… really foreign and odious to spirit; since spirit is precisely the voice of order in nature, the music, as full of light as motion, of joy as of peace…"

And of course, being seen is as much a matter of and struggle with spectatorship as seeing. From birth, all experience is a pentimento without one's necessarily willing it, so much does one become a part of his painting and his painting a part of him.

"A diversion comes along and what do we do? We let it go to waste." Think of it! Every second, and more, at least one diversion comes along.

So what if Caravaggio's original musician was grasping not a love madrigal in his left hand but his erect penis? Isn't what shows at last, the final glaze, the edited version, collected poems, what counts? Who is in charge? Rembrandt, spraying Zeus' gold semen all over Danae, or the villain, vandal, of '85, who washed one third of it away with acid? Perspective lends light years to dark.

"Order presupposes a plurality of elements, and therefore a danger of disruption."

Stars reach out to us like cats' eyes. The chameleon hardly knows what color it is or the octopus its shape as it shape-shifts into flounder, mantis-shrimp, lion-fish, or medusa. Age never comes of age but falls short of absolute realization by alternating phases of ecstasy and exhaustion.

The bough returns to the trunk it fell from in distant winter and cares nothing for its place or nature.

Wayne Sullins

Nature Is Wrong

By midday hundreds of bees are feasting on the carnations. The roads are not paved and the only other way of reaching us is by boat.

In the yard my niece—12, ornery, and slim as a rail—stands with her back to me, holding her right shoe in her left hand. The boat I built for Scratch, I call her, rots upside down beneath the willow. She is humming the Star-Spangled Banner.

Since the girl's mother took her oval mirror and social graces and skipped off to California with a fallen seminarian, I have cared for the child.

She turns and raises her arm to block the sun from her eyes.

"I want you to cut my hair," she says, throwing her shoe at me.

Jill Khoury

Architects, Earthworkers, Agents of Mercy

*Ohio State University Medical Center Hospitals
and Clinics Courtyard, July 29, 2003*

In the morning the workers park just outside the compound, dissolve blankfacedly into scribbles of earth, earth-movers, white coats, concrete, chain link. All day, the shriek of collision accompanies them. It's a symphony of collusion, and the music-makers work it with their whole bodies. Deconstruct a building. Reconstruct a face. Beware, though, of demons lurking in the design. There's one savage utilitarian, grinning like a calliope that plays itself. Don't get too close; he'll swallow you. A sign strapped to his waist says No Smoking, Skating, or Skateboarding, but there are no signs to explain what else is missing: no children, no flowers, no laughing dogs. No one leaping to remove its cargo when the white bus slides up to the curb.

Jenny Browne

The Sunny Side of Amarillo

There are at least two ways to speak the Spanish word for yellow. Locals rhyme it with can-a-hello, optimism included in the $39.99 Day's Inn double where the clerk whispers an explanation for her crying sister, *she wants to get married before she goes to jail so he won't find nobody else but I say he'll find somebody anyways and it'll feel a helluva lot better if they ain't married that's what they call making lemons outta lemonade.* Not exactly but now the sister's pissed and that's yellow too. Further south the double *ll* hooks into a yo-yo wiggling up to the surface like a fish I once caught far from these namesake miles of golden grain. Its lip held a dozen hooks with snapped curly strands of line where don't give in gave out. I'd still rather catch the last thought before any act that lands me sputtering in yellow plastic bucket or in the case of a man from Pennsylvania on trial for poking the bakery aisle: pointer finger tunnels through hundreds of muffins, perfect thumbprints pressed firm into packs of Archway apricot-filled, three mutilated pumpernickels presented as evidence. I think of him in Amarillo as we follow a Mustang with a dented loaf of Wonder sunning on the dash and a hologram bumper sticker that glints *I fear No Beer.* I mean how bad could it be, my last thought before the patchouli roommate again explained her urine therapy and the coward in me emptied, a full glass of *Amarillo*, familiar and frightening as the kind of place you pass through as fast as it passes back through you.

Charles Fort

Brother from Another Planet

for John Sayles

He was born under the low afro stars a toll booth of science fiction and love favorite son and slave of Jefferson. He kissed her wedding dress apparition and drank pot liquor to heal his peg leg. He was born under the low afro stars. They collected taxes on high rise fros wisdom teeth from a nappy negro skull favorite son and slave of Jefferson. There was a clear signal out of his head Hartford seen in a purple choir robe. He was born under the low afro stars. The civil war hero and last man to die boy who swam in a river named heaven favorite son and slave of Jefferson. The liver-lipped newspaper boy genius knew more of this pee world than his teachers. He was born under the low afro stars favorite son and slave of Jefferson.

Driving With Donald Hall in Nebraska

Driving with Donald Hall in Nebraska with a black whiskey flask and corduroy a poem that might have changed the world. The vicar shed his Darwinian cloth and burned a candle to his villanelles driving with Donald Hall in Nebraska. He carved the names of horses, Valentine, lifted a cedar chest and old notes for a poem that might have changed the world. Driving with Donald Hall in Nebraska on a prairie schooner, broke a ghost glass, against the Willa Cather sky, we sang. We sang out for the children and good sleep for lost love letters in tweed vest pockets a poem that might have changed the world. There was a burnt white buffalo carcass, half-slave peasant meth mints a corn row rave, driving with Donald Hall in Nebraskaa poem that might have changed the world.

⚙ Sentence 5

Kevin Haworth

Ethiopian

> *"The first thing we teach an Ethiopian woman is take down the baby from the blanket. Otherwise she'll just carry him around all day and never look at him at all."*
> —*Israeli Absorption Center worker, age 23*

For the first few seconds the siren for the dead is a rising noise. It shakes the jaw, but you stand, back straight. They don't understand the blossoming weight of him, your baby. Carried over long, dry weeks of Ethiopian countryside. With a scent of jasmine like the Song of Songs, and skin

Black as the ovens. He hardly cries anymore.

At forty seconds the siren rings tin-tin inside your head, like a middle-ear infection. Like the one your baby had, when you stepped off the airplane, and the Absorption workers forced drops in his ear. The first of much advice.

He grows like a lesion on your back, this baby. The siren

Recedes, spins down, and it's no longer loud enough to stop you. You cinch the corners of the precious blanket and move yourself and your baby into the street, just before the cars flutter into motion, their engines newly ringing.

Kalev Hantsoo

[Untitled]

The little girl paused. She had never seen that thing on this route, and she had gone this way, to and from her house, many times before. This thing was new. She remained still, waiting for—she didn't quite know what. A full minute passed. Silence amid the looming plane-trees rustling and swaying gently over the alleyway. Shifting shadows jumped and played over the high brick wall against which the new thing was resting. A paper cup skittered and scraped and rolled down the sidewalk, passing not six inches in front of it, buoyed by a playful gust of wind. It was not fear that held the girl there in silence, but rather a feeling of magnetic, of inescapable throbbing power, a gravity that emanated from it in waves—a pounding in the eardrums, a noise so low that it is not heard but felt, like the humming of huge power lines. She took one shuffling footstep toward the new thing.

It opened its eyes.

Hydriotaphia

I

You see that black car across the street? They killed some stray, I think, put it in the trunk.

Yesterday I found a scarecrow in my bathtub. Its long hair was glistening red. Its teeth were falling out.

II

There's a man with no face standing in my closet and another here in my bed.

This one has eyes like the papery rustling of insect husks in the abandoned train depot office in Kilgore, Nebraska.

They stare out of nothing and into nothing.

You see him? (Don't look or he'll kill you.)

III

A dog came into my yard.

I disassembled it but found no traces of tampering.

Children keep throwing balls at the house: I hope they know what's good for them.

IV

In the town of North Wade, Maine, two point one miles due southwest of the junction of Route 228 with the Old Dunn Town Road, there is a dead cornfield. On its western edge lies an uncovered well.

Kazim Ali

The Cemetery at Montparnasse

Each stone is speaking in tongues: *Mon travail est ma priere.* One of the dead is born in my birth year.

An open mausoleum, empty of urns. Blue sky seen through the shattered window.

Near to the gate Sartre and de Bouvoir buried in a single grave. Scattered across the cenotaph an alphabet of stones, dried flowers, museum tickets.

All prayers to our passing.

My stone-tongued mouth.

My work is my prayer.

The Black Madonna at Chartres

The virgin's coat is wood polished black as obsidian stone.

Mary, daughter of Anna, black as stone.

Beaten the veil of Mary paper-thin.

Who I am.

Who I once was.

Wrapped in the veil of the virgin.

Age into stone.

Beneath even this the crypt.

Beneath even that the stone.

Event

Eight white birds, wings tipped with black, flying away.

Snow stretches below into dark. And dark.

"This is the image of the soul leaving," says Catherine. "I sent this postcard to my friends to announce the death of my sister."

The dusty blue sky above the pyramid of Saqqara.

The end of the kingdom. The desert begins.

Near the tomb, a guard lurks. For five pounds he lets me go down into the cold inner tombs.

There, the ancient etchings have been defaced by hieroglyphic grafitti. "First dynasty ruffians," the guard explains, in pieces.

The roof is missing from the temple at the gate. Only the pillars attest to it.

There is a consonant in the middle of my Arabic name that I cannot say.

I mispronounce myself.

At the museum, in a room full of shards, realizing the Egyptian artists *practiced*. Over and over again: a human figure from the side. Two feet evenly placed. Stylized.

No attempt at a retreating figure.

"I love this painting of the cathedral by Van Gogh," says Catherine. "There is no door, no way to get in."

July

We lay down in the graveyard, hinged there.

Emerald moss growing thickly in the lettered names.

You're explaining how trees actually breathe.

Then the green in the moss and trees went up to join the gray in the sky.

Then the gray-green sky came down in breaths to my lips and sipped me.

Ann Howells

galveston wedding

we arrive by ferry crying gulls trail shrimp boats nets upraised wing furled
angels oleander city wedding cake white church rises beyond walkways
carved limestone façade hushed interior groom & groomsmen in shirtsleeves
white bride lifts her lace gown dances barefoot in the surf

Kristin Ryling

I Question If I

I question if I should write with sea pen what memories I extrude from the sponge, the filoplume the heart dapples in russet ink as porferan embellished?

The quill that salientian protests, the tremors no more than hydra.

Aqualine dye tacit on paper, the moods that move as hills or axolotl through the tan frog lifts from the water lily. In the fields beyond the cranefly, the rusting straw shifts in unison. Both, I am, chaff and grain, equal weights accommodating the climate of reason, dying and progression in each breath, I choose only the emphasis. What of the squamous will I proport, any more than the fringillid quote maladies. The rachial in inquest syphen the stain of letters from the flowers butonneire, germinating laquer through the provision of photosynthesis, the blurred root dehisce, applaude shellac, I use them to print the flux text, I am water also and I am tide.

Virgilio Piñera

Swimming

I've learned to dry-swim. It turns out more favorable than doing it in water. There's no fear of sinking because you're already at the bottom, and for the same reason you're drowned in advance. We also avoid having to be fished out by lantern-light or in the blinding brightness of a splendid day. Lastly, the absence of water will keep us from swelling up.

I'm not going to deny that there's something agonizing about dry-swimming. At first sight you'd think of the croaks of death. However, it's different from that, for at the same time that you're agonizing you're very alive, very alert, listening to the music coming in through the window and looking at the worm dragging itself along the floor.

At first my friends criticized this decision. They shied from my glances and sobbed in the corners. Luckily, the crisis is now over. Now they know I feel comfortable dry-swimming. Every once in a while I sink my hands into the marble gravestones and deliver them a little fish I catch in the underwater depths.

Graphomania

All the writers—the great and the inksuckers—have been subpoenaed to the Sahara desert. By the hundreds of thousands this powerful army stands upon the white-hot sands, pricking up their ears—their well-tuned ears—to hear the accusation. Suddenly a parrot comes out of a tent. Standing up straight on its feet it swells up its neck-feathers and with a hoarse voice—it is a very old parrot—it says:

"You are all being accused of the crime of graphomania."

And immediately afterward it goes back inside the tent.

An icy gust blows among the writers. All their heads come together; there is a brief deliberation. The most notable among them steps out of the ranks.

"If you will…" he says at the entrance to the tent.

Right away the parrot emerges.

"Your Excellency," says the delegate. "Excellency, on behalf of my colleagues I ask you: can we keep on writing?"

"But of course," the parrot almost shouts. "It is understood that you will keep on writing as much as you please."

Indescribable joy. Chapped lips kiss the sands, brotherly hugs, some even take out paper and pencil.

"May this be recorded in letters of gold," they say.

But the parrot, coming out of its tent once more, utters the ruling:

"Write as much as you want," and it coughs lightly, "but that doesn't mean you will stop being accused of the crime of graphomania."

The Mountain

The mountain is three thousand feet tall. I've decided to eat it up little by little. It's a mountain like any other: vegetation, rocks, earth, animals, and even human beings that go up and down its slopes.

Every morning I throw myself face down on it and begin to chew on whatever comes in my way. I stay like this for hours. I return home with my body beaten and my jaws undone. After a brief rest I sit in the entranceway and watch it in the blue distance.

If I told these things to my neighbor he'd surely burst out laughing or think me crazy. But I, knowing what I'm up to, see very well that it's losing roundness and height. Then they'll talk of geological disruptions.

This is my tragedy: no one will want to admit that I was the devourer of the three-thousand-foot-tall mountain.

translated by Alexander Cuadros

Rauan Klassnik

Flowers

You're in Vegas and your brain's on tilt. It wants you to rush down into the bars and turn the whores into birds. It says all this filthy light is good and clean. It says you were born to walk with dolphins and dragons, kings and queens with burning hair. There are winners and losers, it says. Don't bring me flowers, you're not the one who's dead. Go for a walk, buy a dress— I'm in the bath, I can feel the canyons, lizards and horses drifting red. And the water is running, and the earth is turning, and in spite of all the doves cooing in every tree the sky tears the earth in a swirl of pink and yellow cactuses.

James R. Scrimgeour

Knuckles

In my dream, I discover a chubby dummy in a treasure chest—a strange toy; when I unscrew his navel, colored tinker-toy sticks pour out—so many of them! When I try to stuff them back in, the dummy cries, does not like the wood, does not want it put back—like Pinocchio, he wants to be a little boy,

a little boy, crying while I replace the stick stuffing, crying, until I tell him he can stay with me—so "Knuckles" (who used to be the fourth step of the old stairway to the attic) becomes my confidante, my companion,

but he lags behind, whimpering under some roots, while I wait for him in the doorway of a rickety construction shed, the shed, built in a clearing, on rock, "Hey, Knuckles," I say, "this reminds me of the rock, the rock on Pine Hill overlooking the state res—one of my favorite spots—where over 50 years ago I would spend time—looking out, you know, just thinking, before the climb down the cliff to swim in the forbidden water."

But Knuckles isn't listening.

Jessy Randall

In the Past, in the Present, in the Future

In the Past

In the past were many dinosaurs, sepia-toned, old and wrinkled, boring, people wore uncomfortable clothes and never said bad words, there was no TV so instead someone sat at a piano and sang SONGS for god's sake. Mr. Potato Heads were made out of actual potatoes and movies cost five cents. Women died in childbirth, babies died all the time, life was simpler and food tasted better, apparently.

In the Present

What is happening in the present? Nothing. Stuff. Well, which one is it? Whatever.

In the Future

In the future there's a little girl zooming around on a trike and the trike glows and the little girl wears special armor and as she spins around and zips and slides she sings a song that hasn't been written yet and now she's on a skateboard and now it's a car and now it's some kind of rocket. And soon it isn't the same girl but another girl contained in the first one. Contained in contained in contained in the first one. Zoom!

David James

The Quiet House

The boy came home to the ticking of a clock. Silence ringing. On the couch, his mother. Cigarettes burning on the table, an empty gin bottle, socks, newspapers. She was dead, he figured. Her skin would fall off soon, her white bones he'd pile in a corner.

But then, she opened one eye and spit.

Peter Conners

Peter Means Rock

Afloat on an ocean of accolades my largest medal will always spell out my geography. This is the city my friends remember to leave: whiskey and winter, twenty-six days of sun. We are all the same, affirmation only a phone-call away. When the polar caps melt the Front Range will be beachfront; miles of burning wilderness extinguished. California is Atlantis deep with veins of post-Apocalyptic gold: Silicone. I do what I can. They do not see me in this garden, my cinnamon arm a transport for peripatetic forms, pulling the weeds, trimming the shrubs, oblivious to Latinate Gary Snyder would savor, deliver. Peter means Rock. My thumb is brown, green, dozens have used it to measure vast distances, hitchhike to sprout in new earthen plots. Place to nose and flick.

Luke Kennard

The Elements

Interview with a Wave

The Wave greets me. I had thought to ask it several pertinent questions such as, "There are more waves now than ever before. Indeed, the adage goes that there are now more waves than there is sea. Is it, therefore, difficult to make a name for yourself as a wave? Could it be said that this has led to an atmosphere of constant pointless revolution and false innovation?" and, "Where does your tide come from? Don't say the moon! That's really pretentious!" and "Do you have any advice—other than give up (!)—to aspiring waves? How has your role as an instructor of younger waves affected your own ebb and flow? Is it a profoundly uncomfortable duality?" However, faced by the Wave's grandeur on so stormy a day, I am rendered speechless and spend my allotted time being tossed around in its backwash, pummelled by tiny stones

Interview with a Breeze

I enter a well-appointed apartment in West London. "It would be hard to deny that absurdity plays a major role in the things you knock over and scatter," I say. "Indeed, an untrained observer might accuse you of knocking over anything and everything without a single guiding principle. Is Absurdism a term with which you are comfortable? Do you wish to distance yourself from the more capricious, fanciful elements of that tradition? Would you like to give me another word for your movement which means exactly the same thing but is, for you, less tarnished by association?" A Venetian blind rattles in the open window. It rattles incessantly, never pausing for a second to wonder how I feel about it. "To what extent do you feel Feminism applies to your work?" I say. "Is your work surreptitiously misogynistic?"

Interview with Fire

I was not looking forward to my first encounter with Fire. His reputation, you might say, goes before him. However, as I poured the remains of the milk into my bubbling, evaporating coffee and the skin of my left hand blistered, I reflected that I had been somewhat misinformed. Fire comes across as a professional who has made the most of the institutional opportunities available in post-war America to build a career. Twenty-two streets of burned out houses attest to the scale and range of his work. Fire, for Fire, is a craft which can be laboured at in the expectation of success proportionate to investment of effort. "Is your work especially autobiographical?" I scream over the collapsing structure. "Given that there are those who criticise you for wilful obfuscation, that is: disguising your woeful lack of substance beneath grand gestures of syntactical disruption and imagistic collage, my second question is this: Please, please will you stop burning me?"

Interview with a Clod

Today we meet an uncomplicated, wholehearted Clod. Gone are the fantastic, illogical flowers and inedible, ugly-looking fruits of his youth. These days the clod is happiest with a clump of dowdy-looking wild grass and a garland of simple, uncomplicated dew each morning. He is even known to use hackneyed devices like "These days..." In an especially gentlemanly touch, the Clod helps me off with my coat, irascibly commenting that back in his heyday he would have gladly helped me off with the rest of my clothes also. Has he, perhaps, realized—given the pathos and tragedy of everyday life—the inadequacy of avant-garde posturing in true self-expression? After a long silence it becomes apparent that the Clod is asleep. "Your work often concludes in paradox," I say. "Is that intentional or do you genuinely not know anything?"

Daniel Grandbois

The Yarn

A skein of yarn was unwound and wound in the shy hours before dawn. Yarn is naturally nocturnal and achieves locomotion by unwinding and then winding. This particular, purple skein would have been fifty yards end to end, had a bramble not caught and kept a long piece of its tail months before. Undomesticated yarn can live up to a year.

Frayed by so many grabbing hands (the rough textures it passed over), the aging yarn pulled itself along, searching for nothing in particular, as that is what yarns do, except the call of almost anyone at all.

"Tell us your tale," a violin spider obliged from its loosely woven web.

The yarn stopped in its tracks and laid itself out, as that is how yarns tell their tales.

"Leaves one unsatisfied," commented the sharp spider. "The ending is too abrupt."

The Log

Once upon a log, a human face was carved. All the more striking as it was carved by a chimp. He'd meant to carve his own face, but his use of tools was limited. Plus, accidents will happen, most always leading to things breaking. That was the chimp's experience, anyway. Just look at how the protruding snout broke off here. And the prominent brow ridge, which was still in his hand.

The chimpanzee buried the brow ridge inside a termite mound where he had gone to look for food, but what interests us now is the log, which was not pleased.

It barked, "Don't stop at the face, *Panzee*! Cut some fists and let's see if you can take it like a man!"

George Kalamaras

Francis Ponge is on Fire

The match is on fire. No, the priest is on fire. No, Francis Ponge is on fire. Fire gives Ponge his body, gives his silk oyster-cream self brilliance. It is a body alive with eclectic thought, with ocean current. The emanating sparrow secretions from his left ear give his body light. It is dark blood-light, like the moment of birth someone who is dying remembers.

The priest is on fire. His black robes are charred parts of Ponge's heart baptizing this child and that. Someone has eased a starter pistol into the rib, Francis Ponge's rib. Someone says, *Stick 'em up! Drop the baptismal fountain! Give me your oyster!* It is not unlike the confusion of a night of unrequited sex. *Give me your oyster* is rebutted with the sweaty sheet-tangle of, *No, give me "your" oyster.*

The university is on fire. The papers are plentiful stars that are, for once, not snobby but in their fragility are about to be human. The brilliant books are alive with wanton ocean depth, burning flood lamps that dim as they enter the mouths of sharks. It is a depth Francis Ponge seeks in the match extinguished in the oyster's rubber limb, an almost holy singe he exacts with the desperate flicking of a pick each evening between each tooth for the charred star and its scar.

Snow-Blind

And so Polina and Bella and I would throw dice and strip. That was the time of poison flowers, of snowberries across the damp, and I would beg a breast from each just to make me whole.

We would read Russian poetry all night as if it were a tragic novel. We tried to mimic Klebnikov's brain. Rail paths through immense snow and the weighty vastness of all that war and space. Sometimes they'd call me *Yuri*, other times *Nicolai*. I begged them to call me *George*. Each of the die contained one blank white side. It was like holding a revolver to your head. If your toss of both die together got nothing, you would strip and the other two would work on you as if you were not yet born.

And so Polina and Bella were beautiful. That was the time of primordial darkness, when my compulsions made me do things in three's, from knocking on wood, to washing the salt, to flicking the light switch even after it was obviously off.

Throw the dice, Polina would say, black strap slipping from her shoulder, as she'd stretch toward me on all fours, cat-like, falling out of her brassiere. *Kiss me where it hurts, my darling*, Bella would beg. *Hold the dice. Shoot across the soft green felt. Let us see the die side white, the warm sluice of all that melting snow.* Did I mention how Polina and Bella were beautiful? Did I describe the vastness of their thigh-tight might?

And so I rolled the dice again and again. And I prayed for *nothing*, absolute and vast, for complete obliteration, for the snow-blind side of the die. The weighty fullness of all that empty space.

Brooke Horvath

The Green One

I live in the subjunctive, a world of if, perhaps, and could have been. I know the name that names my pain, have chained a line straight to it into sorrow's very heart. What is chained to yours? Hint: the last face you see will not be mine.

I confused self-exposure with self-expression, tousled hair with longing, parlor games for come-ons. Boy, girl. I was a guest on a talk show that nobody watched, and once made the evening news. That was me in the background wearing the embarrassing t-shirt.

You are in Paris, Marrakesh, Bali. You are singing pop songs in Serbian, writing poems to painters, drinking wine along the Seine. I am earning wisdom by mail, one mistake at a time. Power tools, holes in the wall, gin straight from the bottle.

Once I painted a wall where paintings were to be hung, large canvases in blues and greens, reds ands grays. They were all about relationship, the painter said. Later I tore down that wall with a hammer and pry bar. It was all about recidivism.

Drunk, I call your lover but can't stop laughing when he objects to my tone. You are far across that lonesome ocean. I am green and you are grown up. What color does that make you?

Yesterday I spent an hour trying to tape your voice messages to me. "Move the blue one next to the green one," the painter said. The blue one; the green one: I love the way artists talk.

Alex Galper

What Abram Grigorievich Did in the Last 10 years

Fell in the garbage pit by the train station; bought two left shoes at the flea market; married a much older broad; triumphed over yardman Makar in a match of domino; got 10 days in prison for stalking some woman while drunk; received invitation from his Israeli aunt; decided to become a traitor and leave; couldn't escape, was forced into a mental institution; got out and left the country; hello America; couldn't stop cursing; abused his wife; admired vodka & local appetizers; washed clients in a funeral home; smoked grass, sold magical herbs ensuring eternal life & youth; divorced; hired hookers, drove a cab; bought a house; married a young chick; got himself new porcelain teeth & a poodle named Prokhor; spent his vacation on Hawaii; once, walked out to mow his lawn—and that was it.

translated by Mike Magazinnik and Igor Satanovsky

Dantes The Hero

After Frenchman Dantes killed famous Russian poet Pushkin at the duel, indignant Polish poet Adam Mickevic challenged Dantes to a duel. Dantes had to take care of Mickevic as well! And so it goes that enraged poets from all over the world kept on challenging Dantes to duels. And Dantes began traveling all over the world in order to kill off prestigious poets like hares on a hunting trip. Pretty soon, he began charging money. In place of dead classics there would come up generations of poets with progressive tastes and different predilections, and literature would blossom wildly taking new directions. As usual, the critics stepped in and noted that after Dantes's departure, the energetic splash of activity would occur in literary life of the country. And so Dantes was proclaimed to be the benefactor of new and avant-garde art

translated by Mike Magazinnik and Igor Satanovsky

Steve Timm

Duck Soup

Go by the names of Peanut and Cookie, and Zeza and Benny, and Sue and Steve. No, it's never all.

Who'll win, that's who. Sense but not in fact. Selection is such a distasteful term when it goes after natural. Decisions decisions. A pineapple tart the name of Carmen Miranda goes by. The next step is learning the names of the parts.

Hindi lessons. What is this? It is a *naak*. I think a lengthened vowel. Just four days and seven (was it) other "tongues." Father time, mother nature. Miracles by definition are orphans. The math be done.

Cheapening is viable. Storm the guitars, strum the gates. Knocknosed we fell in love. History with its rests. The arse or so before the heart. Then we are not cursed?

Let sound be my banner, I do by golly. I go by dolly, daily. The deal is. The good points about denial is a sentence. Hell is a whole number, part of the rational. Paradox is the way asphalt up ahead on a hot day looks like it's got water on it or is. What'll it be gives the status, or location.

Who loses is who we are. Would like to see a head wrapped around the evitable. A head *of* that is. A concession to a third thumb, ghost not born.

Any hoper's final resort is to nonsense. The world a right,—right?

Zentropa

You think you cannot go on. You think it was all designed for you. You think vodka is the wrong god. You think slope and divot and rut are the only world. You think the hours are not of any clock you have known. You think the graves you dug wait for what might have and the two dogs and the cat will sing something instead.

Your proposition is not oblique you think. Stamens and capstans. Unbordered voting blocs perspiring from satiation. Vagabonds *in utero* printing out the diapason of the frontal republic. One ghast of sweet obloquy ears be for. Sentinality played out to an end it could posit.

Serene wipers, still road. Sweat glove jimmy in several jabs. Why they stand at the water's edge in cloud coal dark when no filmer lights the up bubbles. "Up" the cruelest undundancy. Rails is a verb.

What's Up, Tiger Lily?

Now that winter self-dissented and places for knees to be gone down on though it is not as sexual as all that and that worsenings behind walls pretty sure everywhere since here yours too? That was a roughened span howled and et cetera earned. Nevertheless the impulse to pun as wantonly.

At liberty like a corner has it, does it? Maybe every person place name thing should end the same hencetothen? Then. Then. It is a question. A substitute (for) ending.

Neither rhyme nor reason for that sound. It sounded. How ignorant to say so so wolffully. The hell with puns. Am I not right? How unreasonable to think changing (how) out of the question, unquestionably. Being changed (how) being changing (how). Pick up tics. How not new different. Compare *now*.

Thenning, merrily, all one of us at the not very least. Holey.

The Cocoanuts

The land is land by cracky and those who walk on it. These who walk it say land and adjectives and they do pronounce. The wrong moment, a question of technology and the brain in its not quite other failure.

Snakes and rats walk it over moles and gophers there. But it is of course not enough. I don't mean anyone's feet or their eyes in motion on. What kind of glue is that? What sort of terminal? Laminater, laminator. At least I don't believe. In it at last is obvious enough.

It was ours and yours and theirs and now his and hers and yours and but there is no it that it could be its. No big h. Everybody in solitude there. All the Help in the world even its tiniest acre. "Its" like I told you. As if. Tinny.

That and here. Not the very idea or its lack or what the ground feels like in hands if you have them the clods I mean in them. It may be to be done with or employed. A device and its lid. The unfortunate solace.

Geoff Bouvier

Lost Prophet's Song

Call him Qualm. He wants a new psalm. His ear's to a shell, the shell's to the ground, but it's ground, ground, all the way down.

He's Qualm. To him, the world's a maelstrom tossing niceties. Indiscriminately, and more precisely. From foot to foot he shifts: apocalypse/recovery.

Is that a life he's led? Qualm expects to end up pretty dead. Thinks the meantime takes up, what, slack? For distraction, he defines his physique.

Descended from condemning lines of Qualms, he's slight. A mere variation on allotted vocabularies. His position is this: perfectly stationary.

That's Qualm. All pain and bad fight. Instead of the pain-part, he follows the loudest advice. Can't see what it means, but what it says sounds right.

There's a name to fortify yet remedy. It's "Qualm!" At podium-sonority. His fury is boredom-fury. He wants to make a million dollar bet: postponement is all we've got left.

This Postmodern, It Play One...

So. Didn't get wind? Facts were supposed to be in.

Yeah, in *question:* de-sequestered from worn, torn couches.

And out among uninterrupted idiosyncrasies, considering: not one right angle exists in nature. Think about it. Then think it. Lines and curves? Abundantly got. But the rest is our contribution. Folks's.

As for factses, the fact we can't learn new feelings is absolutely reasonable, though perfectly disappointing. There may be disappointment at this felt fact, for instance: if you swum one ocean, you swum 'em all.

And so ours seems a history of cynical extrapolators.

And, and hopeful innovators!

In that skin itself is given to forget... it sloughs it off, and comes replaced. And then? We say one's skin has never swum a certain, unpacifiable ocean.

Not that much has changed. Not as much as it'll have had to have changed.

Flying by the seat of her poetics, a muse is addressing us, Schizophrenia. (Whispering to each other in confidence, explaining moist warmths...)

Meantime, the minute's occupied with sixty second thoughts.

Bill Berkson

Scorsese Point

The night was presumable and like a movie in its salvage. Lasagna fittings
flagged down the fulsome screen as Barb handed him the flabby plaster éclair.
Whoa! Is that Helmut the Sink? A bad joke about city crust and you've just
taken hours on end to wind up seeming. Nothing done is finished, it's all
seen-to any old how, as if allayed. Expand upon this in clitoris time. De-butt
the blouse, the diners far, the stools a-rocking, wrappings cooked in back
of a speed-up van. You part of this payload or what, Sammy? So, to isolate
your strain at day's end, the brass gates spin backward, admit the workings
apparent: road kills and room fucks, idles that stalk and deign to adjoin the
perfected fears. (Ergo, get silly.)

1977/2006

Richard Kostelanetz

Short Novels (with Titles)

Advertising
He relished paternity suits not as threats upon his integrity but as opportunities to publicize his potency.

Betterment
A virgin at twenty, she was a snob at thirty and a spinster at forty.

Apexepa
In the story a that is palindrome is that a story the inn.

Confusd
I'm a man buried inside a man buried inside a woman all wanting to get out.

Die Kunst Der Fugue
He spent the day listening in sequence to all the versions he owned of J. S. Bach's Die Kunst der Fugue, crying every time the last triple fugue ended in mid-phrase, its incompleteness signaling the composer's death.

Hauntin
Obsessed with your face, I see you everywhere I go; I see it everywhere I look.

Ethereal

Better to make us performers seem ethereal, he filmed only our reflections on water.

A Mircle

What was is.

Fortune

Soon after he though himself gay, he had the good fortune of meeting the man with whom he would spend the rest of his life.

Marrying

She married the sort of man who her wealthy parents wanted for her husband and then divorced him in favor of another man who would be, she thought, even more acceptable to them.

Instability

He changed his home address so often that I no longer know where he is, or was.

First Truncated Epic

I
Feeling nothing.

II
Now's too late.

III
Shamanism.

IV
Losing everything.

V
Inbreeding.

VII
Enjoy me please.

VII
Habitually inhabit illegally.

IX
Lifelong pain.

X
Stomach unsettling.

XI
Past perfect.

XII
Generating a conniption.

XII
Going Home.

XIIV
Reconciliation

XV
Conservation of energy.

XVI
Space travel.

XVII
Handshaking every voter.

XVIII
Shock.

XIX
Self-diminishing fasting.

XX
Errant marrieds' adventures.

XXI
Discombobulation.

XXII
Rescuing one's reputation.

XXIII
Winter wore on.

XXIV
Penniless in paradise.

XXV
You understand everything.

XXVI
Down you go.

XXVII
Conjuring contraband.

XXVIII
Connivance.

XXIX
Swiftly intoxicated.

XXX
All-you-can-eat.

XXXI
Undermining civilization.

XXXII
Levitation.

XXXIII
Making no impression.

XXXIV
Unlucky in love.

XXXV
Evening universally advances.

XXXVI
Dreaming.

XXXVII
Love every lunchtime.

XXXVIII
Metafiction.

XXXIX
I'm allover freezing.

XL
Smoking cigarettes continuously.

XLI
Death, I'm ready.

XLII
Saying nothing again.

XLIII
Celebration of sex.

XLIV
Duplicating.

XLV
Astrological forecasting.

XLVI
Necrophilia.

XLVII
Playing stoopball.

XLVIII
Pause.

XLIX
God blessing everyone.

L
Transpiring.

LI
We go on.

LII
Zoom.

LIII
Star treking.

LIV
Unraveling enigmas.

LV
Hand–to–mouth to hand–to–mouth.

LVI
Terminally we dance.

LVII
Feeling nothing.

Another Single-Sentence Story

To write an elongated single-sentence story, I find it advisable to begin
not with a fully detailed outline with each part in the developing narrative
assigned to its appropriate place, but, instead, the nucleus of a motive, such as
the desire to explain how such stories might be written, and then to pursue
the development of that motive until a narrative rich in nuances slowly
appears, the motive thus becoming a kind of scripting machine designed to
generate not just the completion of itself but to fill out its fictional scope,
much as other artworks of mine depend upon similarly strong ideas that
generate imagination as well as restrict it, in addition to creating between
those contrary purposes a tension that is itself esthetically generative, all
these seed fueling sufficient energies to make fullscale works that represent
a surprise to me, their author, who was after all at the beginning familiar
only with the procedural idea that could have, theoretically, generated an
alternative realization, which is to say that even the story told by me here
could have possibly proceeded in another direction to a wholly different
outcome; but, the more I think about it, perhaps the most important point
to make in this context is that it did not, because it could not, because
once I pursued my initial motive, in this case writing within a complex
single sentence a narrative about my procedures for writing complex single
sentences, the number of stories that could be told were not many but one,
only one, which, it should be clear, is what you are reading now.

Daniel Borzutzky

Education Policy Speech

We must support those around the world taking risks to eradicate contracted furrows through legislative measures designed to punish owners of flaking faces who refuse to wage war on the inevitable effects of nature. Our policy must be clear and consistent in its purpose. We must stand by those young women who scream in disbelief upon hearing that once there was a time when wrinkles kept with dignity their crinkled place beneath the eye.

The courage of those multitudes of ordinary citizens who describe their favorite aspect of boredom as that time in the afternoon when millions of people are hopeful that the moon will prevail as it does each night signals the arrival of an entirely different era. We must do everything in our power to foster these views, and to embrace those former experimental poets turned bureaucrats who cut out their own tongues in search of the promised land where words are meant to mean what they mean. Remembering what we saw that morning when those tongues were chopped up and stirred into our morning cereal, we have as clear a responsibility as could ever fall to a democracy: We must do everything in our power to protect our people from those individuals in focus groups who confess that when they picture themselves as fire-breathing dragons, they blow fire out of both theirs mouths and buttocks. (Applause)

This great and urgent responsibility has required a shift in national policy. For the majority of the past century, we have treated the sadism of academicians as isolated cases. Even after an assault inside our own borders—when throngs of nomadic community college professors were

⚙ Sentence 5

filmed flogging pelvis-thrusting administrators on blood-stained sheets atop vibrating mattresses in suburban Red Roof Inns—there was a tendency to treat these sordid scholars as individual criminals, to be handled through law enforcement. These scholars were tracked down, arrested, convicted, and sent off to serve 140-year sentences. Yet behind this act was a growing network of operatives, devoting their days to the service of pedagogy by pulling corpses out of tombs, stabbing those corpses repeatedly until finally the corpses awoke from the dead and sang: We died so that we could be dead, but now that you have killed us we are alive, alive, alive.

Against this kind of determined, organized, ruthless enemy, we require a new strategy with several key elements. These rogue scholars have no boundaries, defend no ideologies, and are unconstrained by accepted rules of conduct. Such an enemy cannot be reprogrammed to meet our criteria. Such an enemy can only be eaten, ladies and gentlemen, and this is the business at hand. (Applause.)

As we speak, ladies and gentlemen, we are marinating in secret cells those tenured members of the Economics, Sociology, and English Departments. Of those known to speak multiple languages, most are now covered in olive oil, lemon juice and garlic, and they will be filleted and skewered before the others. The social sciences and humanities have sustained heavy losses, and they will sustain more.

And we are applying a special sauce. It is one of those condiments that most take for granted but have no clue about its origins. We stored it for many years, and have only recently rediscovered it during a clean-up mission after a graduation ceremony at one of our so-called institutions of higher learning. Sealed in air-tight wooden casks, the ingredients had mixed into a wonderfully flavored concoction which was bottled and quickly became a hot item with the rank and file members of our intellectual-eating brigade.

The first to be soaked in this special sauce were the members of the Honor's Society. Disinclined to participate in athletics, they were not as meaty as some might have liked, but I personally found them quite flavorful, complemented as they were by a full-bodied South American wine.

After that first banquet, we took another essential step in the war on education. This time, in the weeks before grilling, we injected our scholars with a balsamic vinaigrette serum which made them less likely to use words to describe thoughts or feelings. And those who did speak, we stuffed their mouths with cilantro-infused lamb burgers. We thought: if those we eat are well-fed, then we too shall be well-fed. We were correct in this judgement, and when we brushed these free thinkers with sauce, and locked them in our preservation chambers, we sang with glee as moral decrepitude dripped like gravy off their bodies. So proud we were to lick them.

All citizens, regardless of political affiliation, can be satisfied with how we have we dealt with our academicians. And I have been humbled to work with a staff who has shown, in its conduct, the optimism, strength, and decency to capture the residents of our universities, and to serve them in new and innovative ways.

Thank you for your continued support. (Applause.)

⚙ Sentence 5

Raymond L. Bianchi

Theology and Ethics Made Easy

Hanoi, March 6, 2005

Absolute doubt
Before facts that are
Self evidently wrong
And ignored until
The hematoma breaks
And sloshes on the floor
Like a fish out of water
Being filleted while still alive

Phenomenology is a way of creating our own God from wood and stone and plaster and then worshipping ourselves as the divine wind. The openness to our own divinity leads us to do what we can to make ourselves God and ignore questions that get in the way of our objectives.

Transcendental limitation
before the questions that
open up strange paradoxes
in the light of reason
and cold slaps to the face and arms

On Good Friday in many parts of the world bloody processions are held with penitents whipping themselves with chains lamenting the murder of Christ. This also happens in the Shi'ia world when they remember Ali. The dramatic.

Raymond L. Bianchi

of becoming
listen
to
open
door
with wind

vital ecstasy of looking at a painting by Pollock of Krasner or de Kooning
and asking how could America produce these masterpieces? America with
its theology of conquest and conquering the frontier ignores boundaries.
Logically open doors are to be closed. Reading Cole Swensen on a Sunday
morning in Hanoi her words flow out into the perfumed air and people
think that all is lunacy.

Joe Ahearn

Strategy as Artifact

We smoke less now. Though the hells mean nothing to us. Yet still we imagine you lithe and dark, your skin drying to a dusting of salt through the long afternoon. Numb, really. And though in the rain we are still glad, though the woodbine is still sweet to us, what we build is a kind of laugh that doesn't believe in laughter.

=

Though the individual was invented by the French, who needed it for their wars, the individual is actually composed of several geometries; that is, if you plot points along an individual axis, often all the plots are burial plots.

=

Awaken and move to a place where you won't be disturbed. What you are after has a slickness to it. The skin is like liquid there and what lies beneath you can lift away with a spoon. Lay flame along the furrows you've made and what you've discarded give the name of some system.

=

The tea I drink this morning is An Xi. It grew in the mountains of Western China, near the Taiwan Strait. And these mountains, often bluish, resemble pyramids, but the Chinese mountains are redder, and always straighter along the sides than any pyramid.

=

In Nevada one time I saw a pie plate rolling down a hill. The sound it made, metallic but also mushy, reminded me of the sound of the high hat at the beginning of the great Charlie Parker tune, "Romance Without Finance." In modern jazz, the downbeat is often implied but not stated and the musicians improvise around what is essentially a hole in the rhythmic structure. Often in the valleys near my home, you'd see men in working clothes squatting down, rubbing the wet black earth between their fingers. It's a long time now since I've seen such a thing. What I remember now is a kind of sweetness, the good days recurring, my silences like garlands and the garlanding itself something that lay down and slept.

=

The stick is the principal rhythmic device in poetry: all known meters derive from the individual being beaten by one.

Views and Reviews

65 Sonnets

by Brian Johnson

When prose poets gather at conferences to discuss the prose poem, we feel somewhat obliged to define the prose poem. Why? We feel responsible for marking our territory; unlike the purebred dogs, we cannot fall back on pedigree. They'll always get in the show. This presumption leads them to some wonderful self-esteem. For instance, I once taught a beginning poetry workshop at Yale for which there were more applicants than spots. So students had to submit work with a statement of interest and credentials. One student's chief argument was simple: "I've written 65 sonnets." I had to let him in. Would I have been as impressed by a young poet saying, "I've written 65 prose poems"? Certainly not. The sonnet is a greyhound; the prose poem, a mutt. It's all sorts of things: a note from the underground, mulligan stew, the bastard son, garage music, a curio box, a dressed-up anecdote, a dressed-down monologue, a very nice garbage can, a Trojan horse, a dark horse ridden bareback, a funny domicile, a postmodern protofable....

But is it poetry? It's hard to stifle the question. It keeps coming up, especially among verse poets and nonpoets. And I ask myself: is this a good question or a stupid one? It's stupid to the extent that the questioner has no idea what's being asked. For the question is not only, or really, about poetry. It's a question that sits in the middle of every debate about artistic and social change. We all reach the point where we can't keep up, and we feel disoriented, forgotten; we want the new days to be like the old days. We want our new poems to be like the old poems. Modern culture makes Rip Van Winkles of us all. We wake up one morning and discover that we can hardly recognize what we're seeing, outside of us and inside of us. Even Bob Dylan, in his recently published autobiography, admits that he reached the point where he feared his own irrelevance. This, from a man who once had the nerve to use an electric guitar in front of folkies. They didn't even bother to ask, "But is it folk?" The electric guitar was Iago, and the audience a sea of weeping Desdemonas. I can't help but sympathize with the audience. Eros is limited; she only has a few moves—or rather, we remain sensitive to only a few moves, and those were the ones she tried out when we were particularly vulnerable. So even as we become more educated, and more orchestral in our tastes, what touches us may be quite narrow. Our emotions develop before our taste buds, and the taste buds are perpetually trying to catch up. Personally, I suffer from the *Steppenwolf* effect. Every novel I read suffers in comparison to *Steppenwolf*, which staggered my fourteen-year-old heart in a way no subsequent novel can match, even those I recognize as intellectually and artistically superior. Many of our allegiance are based on timing. Maybe if I hadn't been introduced to the prose poem in my second puberty (graduate school), I would think nothing of the prose poem. I might despise it. But I was lost, and it found me.

In general, though, Picasso was right. Everything new is ugly (in poetic terms, the prose poem is relatively new). We could add that everything new is also unartistic, since art has to do with beauty and the traditions of beauty. Just as it takes us a long time to get over our childhoods, it takes us a long time to get over our high-school conceptions of beauty. I still cling to Dylan, to Led Zeppelin, but I have my doubts about the music that came later. Hip hop? Speed metal? Club? They all lack something, don't they? Subtlety? Complexity? Emotional range? Melodiousness? Soul? There's a repressed conservative in the most die-hard liberal, and that conservative is whispering, "The old art was better. The old art was more meaningful." It's why my grandfather says, "You know that poem "I never saw a poem as lovely as a tree"? Amazing. Now *there's* a poem." This view is widespread, even in bastions of progressivism. Consider National Public Radio. How often does their musical programming venture into the twentieth century? Rarely, and even then you're far more likely to hear late romantics like Samuel Barber or Edward Elgar than any of the twelve-tone composers or post-war musicians like Boulez and Stockhausen. And many NPR listeners, though they'd hate to be called anachronists or aristocrats, would probably side with Prince Charles is despising contemporary architecture. The show they love is *This Old House*. Most builders are still making colonials.

Is there anything wrong with this? No and yes. No because taste is a personal right. Yes because the more people who look backward, the more truth and beauty and goodness seem to lie behind us, in some enchanted realm of childhood, milk bottles and rhyme. One could argue that these are strictly artistic questions. *But is it poetry? But is it painting? But is it music? But is it dance?* And that when you say "no," your no is a purely aesthetic judgment. But no is a great multiplier; one "no" represents a series of concentric circles, all of which form our social and political life, where we face similar questions. *But is it marriage?* No, the majority say, a marriage is between a man and a woman. They're not willing to do away with the woman, or do away with the man; they want to be inclusive, and at the same time acknowledge that a lawless universe is a godless universe. *But is it patriotism?* No, you get behind your president in a time of war; there are times when unity is essential, and dissent is inappropriate. It sends the wrong message to the enemy. *But is it strength?* No, strength is knowing what you believe, and never deviating from your course. You cannot be strong and simultaneously mistaken. That violates the unity principle.

These "no"s add up to a way of life, and a defense of a way of life, that cherishes the time-honored values of god, country, family. If it's possible to believe that our national history—and moral history, generally— is a record of pure and uplifting form followed by steady corruption, then it's possible to view aesthetic history as following the same pattern. Then it becomes time to institute the old regime, the old discipline. Artists are not immune to this nostalgic turn (even members of the old avant-garde see the new avant-garde as trivial: a gesture, not a revolution). So most artistic stances, implying if not saying "yes" to this and "no" to that, can be viewed simply as commitments to artistic serious-ness. There is a deep and still-resonating bias in Frost's statement, "Free verse is like playing tennis without a net." I wonder what Frost would think about prose poetry, which has not only gotten rid of the net but is also erasing the lines. Some poets consider that cheating. To me it is not a question of cheat-ing, on the one hand, or observing the rules, on the other, but whether the poem changes the language—in essence, achieves Pound's criteria and makes it new. Art has to mutate in order to live. Mutation is positive, not freakish; it is the mind's attempt to diversify itself, emotion looking for a new set of ducts and orifices. We should admire the mutants among us, encourage them. Prose poets are the X-Men and X-Women. Does anyone doubt that Russell Edson is an X-Man? That Nin Andrews is an X-Woman? *But are they poets? Is it poetry?* To which I say, finally, your question doesn't interest me. We shape things. We have powers. What else is there? Innovators should not be ashamed that we refused the jobs of curators. We're not lost; we're not a threat; there is no pure form that we drifted away from. Let the temple be ruined: that's what happens to temples. The necessary forms and the great beauties are the ones we see in the distance, ahead of us.

Cloud Tablets

F. Daniel Rzicznek. Kent, Ohio: Kent State University Press, 2006.
ISBN 0-87338-868-2

> *Gentlemen, are these verses worth reading?*
> —Ezra Pound

Yes, they are

★

—elegantly made, finely worked, subtle, large in their intentions yet grace-
ful in execution—concerned, imagistically, with light and its absence in the
way the *Cantos* are often about light and its absence; that is, mystical but not
deist: they contemplate the natural object, but find that object not completely
graspable, one that flashes and glimmers and metamorphoses and that often
speaks to us, in the strangest voice, as if out of a cloud.

—poems that begin in that contemporary American style—domestic sur-
reality, the dream life of kitchens and gardens—but something else, something
very interesting, keeps happening along the edges and at the seams.

—altogether careful poems—probably too careful—but they are concerned
with a wildness, a radical lack of moorings and roots, they float and dream, and
in their dreaming remarkable things happen.

★

Look, for example, at "Good Friday," which I take to be one of the best
poems in the book.

A dead smell runs the lawns and the driveways lined with snapdragon buds, ruins the afternoon.

The groundhog in the clover glances from his work and the squirrels freeze like ornaments or branches as the sun comes snowing into the woods.

This pause is no different from the other twenty billion pauses that rush, now and then, through this cramped world.

The deer in the backyards are all glass-eyed imposters, though once something daring and brown was briefly seen as it disappeared.

Beneath a leaden company of clouds that pour weightless across the light, everything shivers, looks up to find the buzzards, who arrived so suddenly, waiting crooked and dark in the dark and crooked trees.

This piece begins, as many of our poems do, in the recognizable world of the suburbs: lawns, driveways, flower beds. But this is not our usual, sunny world. *A dead smell runs the lawns*, a smell so awful that it stops the groundhog in his clover and *the squirrels freeze like ornaments on branches*. But as they freeze, likely cognizant of Good Friday and its symbolism, and even its smells, dead and dark, the scent of the tomb still washing over us, something very interesting happens. *The sun comes snowing into the woods.* The sun comes *snowing*. It overloads the boughs with light. It freezes the branches with a white glare. And everything, all the racket of the woods—the peckings, the songs and calls, the rustlings, the creaks—stops.

But this stopping, this pause at the center of things, this profound noticing of the sunlight-more-than-sun, is both total and ordinary. It happens all the time. *This pause is no different from the other twenty billion pauses that rush, now and then, through this cramped world.*

So now the poem moves its attentions, quickly, with no intervening transitional mush, away from the woods, where the light has come, to the backyard, near the house, sunk in human smells, where *the deer in the backyard are all glass-eyed imposters.* But even here, around the legs of our fakery, we see, if we notice carefully, the brightness of natural movement, for here, in the backyard, even among the imposter wildlife, *once something daring and brown was briefly seen as it disappeared.*

This is the epiphany of flashes, of flights, of small beings moving, quickly, as blur, at the edges of our attention. No greater claim—no big truth, no grand pronouncement—is made. And what we have seen—the glimpse—that we see at all only by looking very closely—is all we get. Because the clouds now come again to pour *weightless across the light.* And now, *everything shivers.* We look up to find the buzzards, attracted by the smell of carrion, the smell, despite the brief, snowy light, of Good Friday, *who arrived so suddenly, waiting crooked and dark in the dark and crooked trees.*

Such complexity and speed. This little poem is only half a page, maybe 120 words, yet it never feels crowded. And it lingers. I find myself thinking about it days later.

★

Of course, not every poem in the book is as good as "Good Friday." Some of the poems based on photographs—"For a Moment," "Gesture"—although beautifully written seem somehow less full than their companions. And the poems of memory and family—"Suddenly I am Child," "Memory System," "Gambling on the Sabbath," "Our Love in a Michigan Gas Station," "The Lucky Ones"—though interesting and surprising in their ways, are limited, to my taste at least, by their intentionality. But even these poems are worth reading, to answer Pound's question, and the rest, well, they are so odd, so wonderfully and surprisingly odd, so deft, so puzzling, so inventive. Here is

"Pecuniary":

> It gives me more to fall away from, and I do, descending past the trumpet sounding toward me, live, thirty years in the past, over the speakers.

> I fall away from my feet, my toes, the whole room and house, away from the land itself, the birds young and operatic in the branches.

> In some green sector of the heart, a radio is playing.

> I fall away from the thought of the soloist's fingers accepting something dark from the concert organizer's pudgy hands.

> A little grey seeps from the black. Flashing in the air: coins with etchings of men's heads, and then paper printed with spider-webbing. On one side, the men again, their faces as if they've just eaten a bad meal, and on the other, a beaming pyramid, a horrible levitating eye.

★

I hope we hear more from Mr. Rzicznek. In the meantime, take a look at his book, and keep an eye on the bushes. Something—beaming, horrible, levitating—is happening out there.

—*Joe Ahearn*

The Area of Sound Called the Subtone

Noah Eli Gordon. Boise: Ahsahta Press, 2004. ISBN 0-916272-81-8

A visit to a local music store can't make anyone an expert on tonic and subtonic sounds. However, the few minutes the store's owner spent strumming his guitar through some progressions gave me at least the momentary experience of a sound that grasps toward resolution. Aggravated, it demands the next tone in order to complete itself. An uneasy place to pause, always on the verge of climax it cannot achieve alone, such is the subtonic. Or, as Noah Eli Gordon entitles this, his second book of poetry and winner of the 2004 Sawtooth Poetry Prize, *The Area of Sound Called the Subtone.*

An excerpt from one prose poem (most here are untitled) gives another sense of the concept, and a fair sense of Gordon's style. "...a space large enough for slips & shifts, the slight nuances of refraction, gold-glints & garlands, Town Square's ineffectual geometry, crossed streets & the crossing of streets, where one defends a sense of direction as insatiable though unsettled, while the numbers won't line up in their proper order..." (35). Whatever else it may infer, the subtone resonates with contemporary experience as Gordon records it. Conclusions are deferred.

Gordon breaks the book into three sections. The first, "What Belongs in the Circle," forms a 12-page-long apparent cento. While Gordon may have authored all the lines himself rather than strictly collected them from other sources, the effect is the same.

> return the question asked
> of a great tragedy upon Latin trees
> moving bodies a vindicated radio

> outside the garden turbulent phenomena
> the sky terrible in wingspan arching over
> an ideal ocean idiotically dented all night the waves
> say marry me to muscle make of me a prime mover
> I'm proud of the lobsters (10)

His vexed juxtapositions twist the imagery through a fast-changing kaleidoscope in which what was thought of the previous line after reading the present line is sure to be mitigated by the next. The dialectical design is intriguing and ever-morphing. Without punctuation and stanza the text thrusts onward with no hesitation. The resulting elliptical effect leads one to wonder whether anything *has* been excluded from Gordon's surrealistic circle (of diurnal existence? of the subtone?), which I think is an accurate surmise. The Circle seems to encompass all.

In the composition of such a piece, fragments attract each other with nonrational sensibility. A cento involves the poetic process of *making* things belong to the circle of itself, the poet playing with patterns of sound, sense, syntactic expectations, absurdity, wit and ultimately, irresolution. This poem and section ends, "O small o of disorder / move me along like we graze here." The disordered o, an erratic circle, suggests continual orbit but also pushes into the next section.

Dense. The writing is dense, in particular this mid-section of prose poems, "Jaywalking the Is." Again the title serves as a key notation with similar resonance. To jaywalk is to walk outside the proscribed lines, which is how a prose poem deviates from traditional prosody. It goes beyond formal line breaks. Also jaywalking the "is," as in *what is*, or some sense of perceived reality, prepares the reader for the transgressions ahead. Gordon will continue to draw the reader outside the lines, whether the narrative line or linear thinking or some proscribed perception of what "is."

Written in single block paragraphs of contiguous non-sequitur that form solid bricks of prose, these pieces offer little room to breathe. The aphoristic nature of many of Gordon's pronouncements compound the effect. A Gertrude Stein epigraph stamps the section: *Sentences are not emotional but paragraphs are*. Gordon either minds or mocks her in writing his, but the idea of emotion expressed in these complex, compressed paragraphs complicates the section for me. So did the specific timeframe Gordon attributes to it, the early months of 2003. Such specificity grounds these poems with a sense of concrete history: something happened during this particular "is." Something with potential emotional impact.

A contemporary reader can't help but think of the invasion of Iraq, and besides the time-frame, portions of text throughout this section support such a reading. "Where are the platinum shimmers in such a catastrophe?" begins one poem that concludes, "The huddlers huddled & I left early enough to pass for an uninvited guest, a kind of music then—the sound of the approaching soldiers: their boots, almost broken in."

Such sporadic topical intrusion doesn't create a general theme but emulates the typical American's experience with the Iraq war as only one facet of daily experience, and only one facet however significant of this speaker's "is." The fact that such reference "appears" at all is noteworthy.

A historical backbeat easily conflates with the personal and relational in these pieces that collect experience from outside the lines. In holistic experience, all such perspectives preside simultaneously, like notes of a chord. Gordon includes the dream world and regularly interrupts his discursive prose blocks with a series of eight numbered "dream" pieces, most in free-line form.

> To say sleep works by accumulation is to disregard the
> weather in my head.
>
> > It makes a genius of the pillow, an apt anthropo-
> > morphic redundancy. (25)

These lighten the page and pace but retain a disjunctive nature. Gordon does not privilege any one mode of experience but questions the dependability of any singular mode to fully express the "is" including the unconscious realm.

> What's in the basement is underneath & I think grand
> pronouncements are a little suspect. Who's in love with the
> dirt clown anyhow? I was clawing at it all afternoon, com-
> ing in without cards, guilty of returning to the same theme,
> grass not being a yard until you project some order onto the
> individual stalks. (78)

A pervasive cynical tone is self-reflexive. Gordon seems as aware of his own attempt to form a yard through gathering individual stalks as he is of the reader's desire to "project some order," to get back inside the comfort of lines. To achieve some resolution.

However Gordon does achieve an approximation of contemporary experience (his) in this section, as well as throughout the book. Societal references appear frequently alongside the particular personal, and his aphoristic style lends an authoritative, even prophetic, quality. Though Gordon confines musicality to line rhythm and sound play, he maintains a subtonic tone and musical reference throughout. In these ways the poems suggest a Blakeian impulse to form a type of "songs of *contemporary* experience," in all that "contemporary" implies in Western literary sensibility.

The final title-section of the book abandons the prose poem for a double crown of modified Shakespearean sonnets, another type of song. This includes the sonnet "x. succumbing to the black dot" whose broken format on the page and desperate imagery manages to cling to 14 lines and requisite final rhymed couplet.

> the loss of space,   blanketing like ash,
> a mirror's indifference.
>
>   borders inherent in the word: fence

Gordon links the sonnets cleverly when not exact. The poem following the one noted above begins "Since when?" The circular aspect of the crown form thematically connects the book's end back to the book's beginning, "What Belongs in the Circle." So too the act of reaching back to historical form suggests the circularity of historical time itself.

Besides their laudable form, these poems' often dark imagery and dystopic tenor evidence the ominous aspect of the subtonic in a societal context when examining what has yet to be resolved. In this format, themes that express the controversial (cloning, the bomb, DNA, cancer, global warming) achieve a tenous political critique without didacticism. Bravo.

> The declaration as opening. As ground or glass is broken,
> so with the cooling, so be it—the core! a slow weather. The weight
> in each word recovered. There were screw holes meant for framing:
> the signs, painted yellow & black. & the amount of notes
> pitched out in a breath, the saxophone's river—its depth:
> there was a city here. here there was a city!   was there a city here?
> They could see what had once been Main Street from beneath the lake.
> . . .we're going down! . . .down. . .we're going down for Christ's sake!

> *(from* "xii: evolution of the order of matter")

Something further can be said about this book and the "subtone." The tangible frustration heard in an unresolved subtonic chord also brings to mind Keats' concept of negative capability, "that is, when a man is capable of being in uncertainties, mysteries, doubts, without any irritable reaching after fact and reason— " Much of what Gordon demonstrates through a suspension of dominant resolution, in "the urge to inhabit the absence of meaning" (79), simulates this abstraction in his poems.

I admire the way Gordon's mind works, skillfully, with sureness and intelligence. To spend time reading these poems—often hard work, to be sure—is to spend time with a careful and probing imagination, to co-inhabit an unsettled yet humanly familiar region in which the poem sounds the boundaries and grapples with what can be perceived in spite of what can't be grasped.

—*Sally Ashton*

Bitterer Pill

A review of *Solution Simulacra*, by **Gloria Frym**.
Los Angeles: United Artists, 2006. ISBN 0-935992-39-1

One wonders when writers will not stare at calamity and answer back in words. The response, whether in the service of protest or witness, is not simply understandable but necessary. After all, while banners are hung and speeches made, someone must record the secret history, or, at the very least, confess that the emperor (and we) are naked.

Still, there is an element to the poetry of protest that is mainly palliative. When direct corrective action or a satisfying resolution seem impossible, the act of writing acts as a balm to lessen the sting of disgust and despair. Reading such work settles the soul and allows a modicum of hope to coalesce around another's words.

The idea of literature as medication wrankles more than a bit, but, as the poet Frym acknowledges, "In order to do what I do, I medicate myself." Perhaps it would be best to judge *Solution Simulacra* in terms of how efficiently it fulfills this role—by marking how many times I agreed with the poems. But "I'm drunk (with wine, poetry or virtue, as you please), and so are you," hardly seems grounds for comment.

That these poems are mainly prose seems right. The passion of the polemic won't organize into nicely beautiful verse; Frym's voice runs out unabated. The majority of the non-prose pieces spread across the page more like wild grass across a field. Containment and rigid structure are antithetical to these poems.

And the poems address the call to writing during calamity: the "[t]roubled trope for incomparable times." Although "poetry [may] accept all subject matter," Frym admits that "writing…craves beauty." Yet, as the poems point out, "[m]uch of the world imagines death as beauty," and that the present not so beautiful moment is something from which language must protect itself.

In times such as these—which must mean all time, because this moment is all too familiar—the real test of the poet is not how much the reader agrees, but how much the poet gets right. And there is something about beauty caught up in this "rightness." Beauty which is idealized into voluptuous, seductive thought will not do, though wouldn't it be pretty to think so?

Frym critiques the imposition of something like a beautiful idea in these poems. This is, of course, the "solution" that looks and feels and seems like a solution, but instead led to the calamity that inspired this book.

If beauty is voluptuous, it is a fleshy beauty—made of flesh and blood, and flesh and blood are messy—then they become even more messy when one tries to replace that very specific flesh and blood with an idea. Just like the child's sentimental and unrealistic idea of a dog as something to be walked and loved (surely dogs are hunters and workers, more bomb-sniffers than toy pets), flesh and blood cannot be sentimentalized or demonized without dire consequences. In a poem this leads to artistic failure, even if we agree with the polemic. And, as Frym's poems insist, in the world of dreadful action and fatal resolution the consequence has always been bloody and final. This is a bitter pill that neither medicates nor cures, but sticks in the throat.

—Brian Brennan

Concentricity

Sheila E. Murphy. New York: Pleasure Boat Studio, 2004.
ISBN 1-929355-16-5

Throughout her poetic career, Sheila E. Murphy has been known for her innovative prose poetry. Her 1997 *Falling in Love with You Falling in Love with You Syntax: Selected and New Poems* features no less than 62 prose poems, about 40% of the book as a whole. Her debut volume, *With House Silence* (1987), consists entirely of what Murphy has termed "American haibun," prose-paragraphs followed by a single sentence or fragment without a period. *Concentricity* is composed entirely of single-paragraph prose poems, only a few of which exceed a page, and American haibuns.

Some prose poems in *Concentricity*, though not precisely offering linear arguments or narratives, can be read as covering a particular subject. For instance, "Matches," an American Haibun, begins with a description of the camaraderie of cigarette smokers, probably by a non-smoker, and includes how people are seduced by the glamour culturally attached to this deadly habit: "I still feel the trickle of what was sexy and desirable in film, those hats that frame deceptive eyes. The cool exhale is actually a hot" (48). Full of subtle pathos balancing the humor of Murphy's unusual word-combinations, "The Sorting Process" involves the problem of sorting such notions as aesthetic "craft," "credibility," and "success":

> She said evidence of craft within a person had its edges.
> She said color of the tight vest ought to be some kind of
> a criterion but that would never likely fly. I wondered for
> a moment about credibility I had all along assigned to her.

> I wondered how derivative I might be, standing on wet
> pavement, trying to construct some permaculture from the
> spatty pools and shiny leaves and soggy things once thrown
> away. What constitutes success? (18)

Murphy goes on to parody newspaper hype and "tanned announcers" for their superficial answers to her serious question, as well as the tendency of "uneducated people" to appropriate the "ideas" of "great minds" in the service of apparently narrow goals. In certain circumstances, she must acknowledge that "ardent prejudice" manages to "sell well," and so the terms of worldly success may have little to do with "lives that prove their good intentions."

Following a practice that Murphy has undertaken at various points in her career, several texts present "portraits" of individuals—somewhat less abstract than Gertrude Stein's but far from ordinary character sketches. In "The Solo of Desire," she describes a man's refashioning of his daily life after a dramatic change: "How simple, when a thing is over, to refashion it. Quiet seemed a viable, long-term solution to the years of being loved in that conspicuous full way that prompts a form of rage no one can understand" (24). "Temp" registers the enervations and "numb safe drone of repetition" faced by temporary office workers without insulting us with the obvious: "She logjams her way back to reflexes rumored to be natural" (21). "She Was Losing Hair," "Her Docile Art," and "She's So Specific" are other strong prose poems in this vein.

Though Murphy's language is always fresh and surprising, the texts I have mentioned thus far are much less referentially elusive than most of the work in *Concentricity*. One point of entry into the more "difficult" prose poems is to become attuned to Murphy's particular musical effects. Here are the opening sentences of "The Meta-Ecstasy Sells Short":

> Each subtraction first convinces that tradition's a baton.
> That fig leaf over deals not what they used to be. Throngs'

⚙ Sentence 5

Recollection. A temerity goes father limp. Men in the dream thick with repair. The state of dis-. Sunbathing in the very much unglued soft water. Rebels leaven in wall sockets where some spaces in between allow the luxury of eccentricity. (49)

The first sentence features the slant-rhyme of "subtraction," "tradition's", and "baton," whereas the short words in the second one includes an interplay of varied "e" and "o" sounds, as well as two initial "th" sounds that connect with the opening word of the next fragment. A rich crossing of "a," "e," and "I" sounds surrounding a single long "o" adorns the fourth sentence, and some of the "e" and "i" sounds resurface in the next fragment. "Temerity" is the first of six words in the prose poem with "y" endings. The crossing of vowel effects plays against adjacent words possessing assonance like "Rebels leaven" and a later sentence, "Fast forward taxes bags under the eyes."

Finally, toward the end of the text, many "l" sounds appear in various locations within words: "Forelockable as seat belts. She rubbed the sitcom so oblivion first faltered on two wheels. The ultimately selfish guest erased a continent depicted pale eye blue." Note how the "l's" (except in the case of the nearly rhyming "wheels" and "pale") are part of a syllable including a hard consonant, such as "b." My elaborate account of sound-effects in a relatively brief number of words does suggest that a great deal is going on, yet it is not programmatic in any discernible way, as a rhyme-scheme would be.

I am not content, however, to suggest that analysis of Murphy's poetic music is adequate as a single approach to most of her work. One should chart how resistance to meaning and opportunities for rapport between and among sentences press against one another. The opening sentence of "Vault," "We have bootlegged matching body chemistries," presents an amusing hyperbole indicating the strong desire for a sense of unity between two people, something so challenging to achieve that it must be stolen: whereas the following sentence contrasts in its implication of competition among "strangers" in an opulent resort: "I hear this is a suites hotel where each one's neck and neck with strangers capable of Rolfing or deciphering Egyptian characters" (16). Even if this discord can be smoothed over by personal warmth ("The lapdog of our sensibilities calms strangers"), the text soon breaks into diverse perturbations:

> Equally, viscosity deranges pulp and garden tools and heavy-armed equipment. She said that he reminded her of slim pond prose. She was wearing six-plus pounds of tone. Levels impulsed their way to my cravat. I simply soloed out of reach and madcap heresy just out of strict conformance. (16)

Murphy "vaults" from human psychological concerns to pondering liquid's physical effects on objects and substances, *except that* it is easy to read "viscosity" as a trope for a loss of psychological flexibility, excessive emphasis on one's defenses against perceived dangers, and a "deranging" of technology's positive potential for natural growth. The discourse of insult ("slim pond prose" or scum, as opposed to seaweed) is an example of such psychic "viscosity," and the "six-plus pounds of tone" that someone "was wearing" conveys a sassy attitude much more than makeup or sun block. What kinds of "levels" can impulsively fixate on the speaker's tie? Could they be levels of "tone"—for example, supercilious class analysis of sartorial signifiers? The speaker's withdrawal from this damaging situation is accompanied by the posture of a zany trickster who challenges established hierarchies by eluding ordinary sense, just as Murphy turns the noun "impulse" into a past-tense verb and the adjective "madcap" into a verb. She also transforms "conformity" and "performance" into the nouveau portmanteau "conformance."

The end of the prose poem swerves in a new direction: "It takes several spare monks to jumpstart a religion. Several under-recognized hewn minds. Cane sugar in sufficient quantity to unseam the emotions cantilevered in teased tragedies" (16). Self-protective "heresy" has given way to the recharging of a religion's "battery," perhaps through innovation. The idea that those "spare monks"—the adjective indicating both leanness and underutilization—have focused "minds" that lack sufficient recognition is important, because their very lack of prominence in an oppressive ("cravat"-mocking) environment may give them the perspective needed to freshen a collective imagination. "Cane sugar," a trope for any potent sweetness, seems to detach followers from "emotions" that would push them to other paths (than the religion in question). That these emotions apparently exist *within* "teased tragedies" does not tell us whether religious devotion would deliver them from misfortune or would comprise allegiance to some tragedy, like a noble sacrifice. "Teased" could either signify comic dilution through mockery or an establishment or refinement through combing or polishing. This final ambiguity suggests how forms of persuasion can address differing emotional situations and how language reflects these possibilities.

"Vault," a title which does not appear in the text, includes the connotation of spiritual aspiration (a cathedral's roof structure), a crypt, a place for the storage of money and jewels, and the equally aspirational verb for leaping, which could indicate the movement from sentence to sentence. One may ponder which phases of the prose poem reflect emotional uplift, spiritual death, or action designed to protect one's capital.

What, then, should we make of *Concentricity* as the title of Murphy's book? Culled from the title of one of the prose poems, which begins with the felicitous sentence, "Installations house imaginary stallions" (17), it "nouns" something that, in standard English, can only be an adjective or adverb, thus decentering or recentering language. Could this title be propounding a poetic faith in the Coleridgean "unity in diversity" that ballasts the old American New Critical aesthetic? Is the book a concentric *city* of different neighborhoods bound by a central government? It is doubtful that Murphy would share Coleridge's *thematic* emphasis; the title could be a joke or a jovial dare. (*See how far you'll get if you look for concentricity!*) On the other hand, "concentricity" may signify the overlapping of different linguistic and musical scales whose cognitive and affective "center" is the prose poet's perceptual focus, immersed in flux, (as suggested by "Concentricity's" last sentence, "Small temple's ice changing its chemistry to water running down the stain glass windows"), and her deep fascination with what words, phrases, fragments, and sentences can do to and with each other when juxtaposed in small, medium, and large units.

—Thomas Fink

In the Heart of the Heart of Another Country

Etel Adnan. San Francisco: City Lights, 2005. ISBN: 0-87286-446-4

Mid-American Chants

Sherwood Anderson. Florence, MA: Quale Press, [2006].
ISBN: 0-9744503-4-0

Etel Adnan is the author of *Sitt Marie Rose*, a novel about the Lebanese civil war, and, among others, the poetry collections *Arab Apocalypse, In/Somnia,* and *The Indian Never Had a Horse.* A Lebanese-American whose work has been praised, in the words of Juliana Spahr, for its explorations "of war and the female body," Adnan here takes us in seven short texts from Beirut to Bay-area California, from Benghazi, Libya, to the deserts of T.E. Lawrence, from a Thelonius Monk concert to the beginning of the 2003 war with Iraq to explore what the modern world has made of her and, by implication, of us all. As she describes herself, "I am both an American and an Arab and these identities are sometimes at odds with each other, not every day, not even often, but once in a great while I become a mountain that some terrifying earthquake has split" ("Present Time").

Readable as a memoir in the form of a journal, *In the Heart of the Heart of Another Country* takes its structural cue in five of its seven sections from William Gass's story of (roughly) the same name, employing his section headings and, in Adnan's words, "'answering' them." These answers, she tells us in a helpful introduction, speak of people caught up in the catastrophes that have defined the last century of our history and of how, "contrary to what is usually believed, it is not general ideas and a grandiose unfolding of great events that most impress the mind [. . .] it is the uninterrupted flow of little experiences, observations, disturbances, small ecstasies, or barely perceptible discouragements that make up the trivialized day-to-day living." "To Be in a Time of War," a response to the invasion of Iraq composed almost exclusively of infinitive phrases, provides an example:

> To go to the dentist early in the morning then drive back and come home. To lie down, waiting for the news at noon. To have a headache. To be impatient. To vomit the war. To greet the fog with joy, with tears. To find tenderness in stones. To greet Sarah Miles, with tea, with cakes. To miss the news. To chat. To say goodbye. To start packing. To forget the war. To never stop thinking about it. To ignore the beauty of the day [. . .]

In the Heart of the Heart of Another County offers itself as fragmented, subjective meditation. Eschewing pedestrian coherence for subterranean connections of the sort that bind the paragraphs of Gass's ur-story or the entries in Thoreau's journals, Adnan speaks in seeming non sequiturs of politics and love, identity and history, memory and misery:

POLITICS

In my view Yasser Arafat existed only on television. For the people, he was in New York. An Arab in New York spoke of Palestine. His gestures were those of an Indian Chief. He was the real leader of a real country. He was also the possible leader of a possible country. Angels covered with blood were flying in the American sky. New York is the deep canyon of the soul.

Meanwhile Beirut moans and burns. But not a single voice is to be heard on behalf of the torn muscles, blinded eyes, cigarette-burned faces, vertebrae broken with an axe . . . It is as if Beirut has become an anatomy treatise that one reads in some dark corner of hell.

FINAL VITAL DATA
On the way to extreme consciousness one encounters, like on a high road, pain. Then, one backs up, turns around, and goes home.

What we call a loss of memory, the impossibility to remember, is in fact an inner deafness, thinking being separated, by some kind of a curtain, from the inner ear; it is a power failure [. . .]

Although she classifies *In the Heart of the Heart of Another Country* as poetry, Adnan refers to her often challenging, sometimes baffling, and occasionally brilliant book simply as the result of "a particular attraction to paragraphs." Similarly, Sherwood Anderson saw *Mid-American Chants* not as poems or prose poems but as "songs" (or, in a letter to Waldo Frank, as "things")—and like Adnan he wrote in part to protest the incoherence and fragmentation of the soul recent history had introduced into the world.

Published originally in 1918 after its furious composition in early 1917, the collection has usually met with a dismal critical reception. Irving Howe found the poems "fuzzy" and "self-indulgent," concluding that "they are not poems," while the critic David D. Anderson has described the collection as "not only trying, but tiresome." Indeed, Walter B. Rideout is correct when he observes that "Anderson was a better poet in prose than in verse"—as Anderson's next book, *Winesburg, Ohio*, would demonstrate—and *Mid-American Chants* will interest many readers more as evidence of Anderson's search for a voice and a vocation than as a fully accomplished book in its own right.

Written in free verse and prose, the forty-nine poems collected here (Anderson's only poetry save for 1927's *A New Testament*) reveal a debt to both the Bible and to Walt Whitman, as the concluding stanza of "Chicago" perhaps suggests:

> Look upon me, my beloved, my lover who does not come. I am raw
> and bleeding, a new thing in a new world. I run swiftly o'er
> bare fields. Listen—there is the sound of the tramping of many
> feet. Life is dying in me. I am old and palsied. I am just at the
> beginning of my life.

If not every poem works to forward the book's overall message, that message is clear: Americans have lost a golden agrarian past and, mired in industrialism, have forgotten how to sing, by which he means to commune, to live. As Anderson puts it in his Foreword, "I do not believe that we people of mid-western America, immersed as we are in affairs, hurried and harried through life by the terrible engine—industrialism—have come to the time of song," adding that men are, however, "awakening. Like awkward and untrained boys we begin to turn toward maturity and with our awakening we hunger for song." Lonely and lost, Americans need a bard to lead them into a better tomorrow, and Anderson writes that he has "dared to put these chants forth" only because he is convinced that "in secret a million men and women are trying, as I have tried here, to express the hunger within," making *Mid-American Chants* a kind of how-to book and Anderson a kind of prophet or culture hero.

I have noticed the collection's tedium and vagueness—difficulties that sometimes arise when one attempts to say the previously unsaid, the previously unsayable. Yet these are faults most noticeable when the book is read straight through rather than a few poems at a time. Taken individually, the poems are frequently striking, specific, and beautiful:

> Her eyes are like the seeds of melons. Her breasts are thin and she walks
> awkwardly. I am in love with her.
> With her I have adventured into a new love, in all the world there is no
> such love as I have for her.

I took hold of her shoulder and walked beside her. We went out of the
  city into the fields. By the still road we went and it was night.
  We were long alone together.
The bones of her shoulder are thin, The sharp bone of her shoulder has
  left its mark on my hand.

         (from "The Stranger")

Not long ago, the critic Jed Rasula asked what it means "for a society to
embrace, as its cultural *mythos,* a body of work that celebrates collapse, decay,
attrition, and malaise?" It is that mythos that Anderson sought to revise, just as
it has been Adnan's task to describe the world that has resulted from our collective failure to live out that revision.

         —Brooke Horvath

At That

Skip Fox. Tokyo/Toronto: Ahadada Books, 2005. ISBN 0-9732233-6-7

There is something odd about the current fascination with author's journals, sketchbooks, rough drafts, and writing processes. The desire to see writers
reveal false starts and wadded-up drafts is perhaps a human reaction to con-
firm that writers are no different than anyone else, but are merely more persistent than the vast majority people who claim they "have a book in them."
This year saw the appearance of two posthumous tomes from Elizabeth Bishop
and Jack Kerouac, two of the modern canon's celebrated masters; Alice Quinn's
edited collection of Bishop's drafts and fragments, *Edgar Allan Poe & The Juke-
Box* (Farrar, Straus & Giroux, 2006) and Kerouac's *Book of Sketches* (Penguin,
2006) were both critical successes, and revealed that these favorites of English
literature professors across the North American continent were just as human
as the rest of us, delivering bum line after bum line, bad idea after bad idea, and
that they worked at revision with a monastic attention to detail.

To further feed the desire to see the drafting process in real-time, this year
also saw the debut of QuickMuse.com, where two publishing (*neè* academic)
poets are given a surprise prompt and fifteen minutes to complete a finished
poem. Each writer's keystrokes are logged to reveal how the poem takes shape
during the competition and archived online—the ultimate in slow-motion
replay. But in our zeal to see that the emperor has no clothes, that the person
behind the curtain is merely a person and not an all-powerful wizard, we often
encourage those who need no encouragement—for we must bear the bum
notes and melodies of those whose notebooks aren't worth reading for pos-
terity's sake or for insight into artistic craft, but make for delightful diversions

nonetheless. And thus, we have Skip Fox's first full-length collection. What Fox has given us are the seeds to our own poems, as we never know what we will encounter when we read around these pages other than incoherent connections that we ourselves complete much later, after putting the book down and moving on to something else.

The conceit of *At That*—if it can be called a conceit—is that each piece is dashed off like a diary entry, numbered in what seems to be no particular order, and thus the book only makes sense if read randomly. We are supposedly given insight into the writer's brain as it unfolds and confronts life in all its gory details. Bad puns, make-believe dictionary entries, sardonic reflections, sarcastic recommendation letters, lyric and experimental poetry, witty sex jokes, Post-It Note punditry and good old American navel gazing are all interspersed to create a non-narrative in the spirit of the L=A=N=G=U=A=G=E poets, the French Oulipians, and the modern day flarf and spoetry (spam poetry) movements. To read this book by starting on the first page is a mistake. And so is calling it prose poetry. Or poetry. No, this is a textual tour de force, a commonplace book merged with an outboard brain, a hipster PDA, a reprinted Moleskine without all the messy revision marks.

In this regard, Fox is heavily influenced by and draws upon the traditions of Burroughs' cut-ups, Brautigan's absurd metaphoric inversions, and Dorn's deceptively intense clarity. Fox gives us his meditations laid bare, a running stream of consciousness commentary on the mundane and sublime, giving us a glimpse into the working and non-working mind of a writer at work and rest. This is Zen monkey mind at its distracted fullest, zipping and zinging from association to association. Fox moves at a kinetic pace, twisting language as he crams alliterations and allusions and wry observations into prose lines so densely packed that it is difficult to read between them, as here, in this passage from entry 572, 968 (that's two separate entries; supposedly he went back and added something):

To do anything with due consideration, forget what you are doing (Way of Samurai, Silence of Stone, seven), Thomas and Judah hanging out in the withered dawn by a lamp-post, needle through the nose of an angel, bass bellow of city stretching, barely audible, and so forth, the brick so lively this time of year, what you waiting for, as she said, the man who heard spiders bark is an obligatory phrase in this sentence now that it is so constituted as anything else, i.e., once you have seen dawn through Jonas's eyes it will all come clear in its terrifying nearness, another circumcision "error" (I just came in for a haircut) dogs barking down the street (and look at what happened!), world of distraction, if this were a Jane Austen novel you wouldn't be reading it, you'd be reading something else.

The wall of sound and sight and ideas that Fox throws at us are overwhelming, a cacophonous litany of observational impressions that it is nearly impossible to carve out space to breathe. While many turn to poetry for insight and reflection, Fox instead acts fool, revealing the absurdity of modern life's constant media-saturated comfort zone feedback loop.

The entries are often overly entertaining, and I found myself laughing aloud at some of Fox's verbal maneuvers, especially a recurring "Sure Shots" gimmick, where he wraps advertising jargon around to-do list entries, witty commentary, and philosophical double entendres—"Wake up and smell the smegma," for example. Fox loves toilet humor—the kind of humor found in Kevin Smith films featuring Jay and Silent Bob—and combined with his willingness to record his unabashed reactions to the world unfolding around him, this makes for a potent combination.

The press kit materials for the book proclaim that Fox, "with the concern of an entomologist, presents passages sprawling and pinned in a shadow box of observations and odd lots." The last time I checked, entomologists need to kill things to study them fully, and by pinning down his impressions with such alacrity, Fox appears to trying do in experimental narrative itself. It is easy to dismiss Fox's effort here as no more than the ramblings of a self-indulgent linguistic experimentalist and think that, like the urinal depicted on its back cover, the book deserves to be flushed—Duchamp be damned. But in doing so, you'd miss a frustratingly mad read.

This book not book what is a book but a collection a mad stumble a beehive of meaning which I built this morning out of raw wood and ball joints joists bursting to hold not hold unhold and divest itself of what and then some is an interesting take on the phenomenon of revealing what it means to be a writer. If only the reading public would take notice. But they won't. It's too dangerous. Better to play it safe with Bishop and Kerouac—writers your English professor told you were good. Leave Fox to those who like to play with matches. We like to keep a good thing to ourselves.

—*Matthew W. Schmeer*

Meteoric Flowers

Elizabeth Willis. Wesleyan University Press, Middletown, CT: 2006.
ISBN: 0-8195-6813-9.

"This I, this me, I'm speaking from a book." This sentence opens the prose
poem, "Primeval Islands," found near the end of Elizabeth Willis's newest collection. "That brain that taught me delicious things, forgivable trains, a signal
business," the poem continues. These two sentences, opposing "this I" and "that
brain," represent a fundamental dynamic in Willis's work: the tension between
the expressive self and the discursive brain, a brain that is and isn't part of the
self—a brain that is always, to some extent, Other, "that," outside of the notion
of the feeling self and involved in its own sort of "signal business." Or, perhaps,
the book itself is "that brain" through which the expressive self is filtered, the
brain that teaches delicious things?

Wallace Stevens wrote, in "Imagination as Value," "There is more than the
romantic in the statement that the true work of art... is not the work of the
individual artist. It is time and it is place, as these perfect themselves." The turn
to Stevens to understand Willis's willed "dissociation of sensibility" in this collection is not arbitrary: the collection's epigraph, "Poems are meteors," comes
from Stevens.

Where T.S. Eliot lamented the "dissociation of sensibility" as the estrange-
ment of thought and feeling in English poetry—based on his assumption that
the fertile ideal blending of them can be seen in the work of metaphysical
poets like Donne—*Meteoric Flowers* accepts such a dissociation and seeks ways
to locate poetry in the chasm between the two. If the Enlightenment was for
Eliot the moment in which the sterile effects of the dissociation were most

manifest, it is, for Willis, the time during which poet and botanist Erasmus Darwin, Charles Darwin's grandfather, produced writing that is "an eerily apt model for riding out the inter-discursive noise of the early twenty-first century." Willis pays tribute to Darwin's 1791 *Botanic Garden* by using his text to form the titles for the poems in her book.

While the book is not directly about botany, the tropes of flowers, foliage, and buds appear frequently. The poem, "Bright O'er the Floor," begins with botany—"Suddenly the daisycutter someone was waiting for" – and ends with it – "We're rowing like Greeks before those trees turn to treason, erased of all their writing." Often, as in the latter instance, these botanical tropes allude to writing; more often, they are made to coexist with mineral, even synthetic, images, such as the "luxe enamel" and "colorless glass" of "The Portland Vase" (quoted below). Animal, vegetable, and mineral merge in a line like this one (from "The Oldest Part of the Earth"): "We're only clay: blossom machines." So, if not exactly inter-discursive, how does the "signal business" of the prose poems in this collection fill the chasm between thought and feeling? And do the interaction and surprising juxtapositioning of the animal/human with the mineral ("meteoric") and the vegetable ("flowers") have anything to do with that?

"The Portland Vase" may help to get at these questions:

> Dawning at the shoulder, I beg to add this foliage. A butterfly placed to resemble a country. The grove to whom you bring a cloak, the vital air you see through. Not moist or dry, not clay as we know it, her cheek of luxe enamel, colorless glass where the capital has fallen. Accidental arguments, described as mysteries, pull the needle in the dark. The law stands or rests, its fame in flower, its leaf-like warmth. To present a real person, sitting on a book, the torch must be in someone's hand, abandoned to its latitude, hungry of shade.

Willis's treatment of a "still life" here is reminiscent of "the rose is obsolete," William Carlos Williams' heuristic poetic rendering of a Juan Gris collage in *Spring and All*; in the prose following his poetic exercise, Williams says of Gris's process:

> Things with which he [Gris] is familiar, simple things – at the same time to detach them from ordinary experience to the imagination. Thus they are "real" they are the same things they would be if photographed or painted by Monet, they are recognizable as the things touched by the hands during the day, but in this painting they are seen to be in some particular way – detached.

For Williams, the Imagination was a tool not for copying reality, but for re-creating it, changing its venue, as it were. Williams' Imagination and Willis's book-as-brain are aligned in their acceptance of dissociation and detachment; for both poets, textuality is the means for filling the distances between what is dissociated, be it the internal and external worlds, the subjective and the objective, the cognitive and the affective, or the notion of the "I" and the "inter-discursive noise" of the text. The filling is not about unifying these dissociated entities or processes or modes of experience; it is about showing what these dissociations generate—flowers growing from the ungiving surface of a meteor, or a flowering of words whose materiality has both the density and potential energy of meteors.

Willis organizes her book into four cantos, or groups of titled prose poems, with short lyric poems as interludes, claiming in doing so to be reversing the format of Darwin's text, with its poems interrupted by prose notes; equally, one might see her project as a descendant of *Spring and All*, where one no longer has to argue with Eliot and "the Traditionalists of Plagiarism" who call for transparent "realist" renderings and the objective correlation of image, feeling and idea. After all, Willis's final poem, "Ferns, Mosses, Flags," begins by observing, "We all live under the rule of Pepsi, by the sanctified waters of an in-ground pond." Under such rule, a postmodern given, the vegetation that strains to flower by the road to the contagious hospital, near patches of standing water, are "uncertain of all/save that they enter." Similarly, "Ferns, Mosses, Flags" ends with the uncertainty of "this I" who tells the reader, "I read the picture and did what it told me, ducking through the brush with my tablet and pen, following some star."

—Ellen McGrath Smith

The Night I Dropped Shakespeare on the Cat

John Olson. New York: Calamari Press, 2006. ISBN: 0-9770723-3-9.

> Our perception of the world is an act of faith based on fragments,
> images carved out of the air by poets.
>
> —Olson, "The Fabric of Fabrication"

Throughout John Olson's work, there is poetry that tends to reconfig-
ure meaning by associating words unaccustomed to appearing in the same
utterance: "I was about to nail the harmonica reservoir to my necktie when
I realized life is a palate soon scripted by a thermometer. It is not invisible to
perpetuate a sample of this"—is just one example. Olson is not the first poet
to use associative dissociation (my term), but he is definitely good at the tech-
nique, expert at showing the reader "the bright succulence of words." So it is
a pleasure to read a text in which a writer re-strings words to make us rethink
the *reality* of language. To be sure, Olson's poetry works the reader, wakes
up the mind, and makes one wonder that someone first named an object or
action, that someone once sculpted those "bits of air called words." And if, centuries ago, a person gave name to a thing, then why not the poet now? Why
not pry word from meaning or give expression to something seemingly non-
sensical that may after all make sense? This is what poets do in the realm of
art.

Outside of art, in our political rhetoric for instance, words may be released
into the air free of their usual and expected meanings—words like *detainee* or
interrogation. However, we call this deception, dishonest use of language. In

some realms, then, the way one constructs language and meaning is critical. Sometimes a man who uses language imprecisely or nonsensically brings about human carnage. That is why it pays to be thoughtful when choosing a profession that involves expertise in language.

Olson has chosen well, and he has executed a creative text that not only offers the remix of language but also looks at how we construct and use words, imagery, narrative, and poetry. In reading the poems, one begins to wonder, shouldn't words always be formed on the basis of the function of the things they name, as in the word *agitator*: "Perfect name. Perfect correspondence of word and function."

More than once, Olson directs the reader's attention to "events sequenced in time [that] hold the air in place," or narrative. What is the right form for one story or another, especially if we believe that "there is reality in shape, shape in reality. Fables, blisters, flint." Moreover, Olson brings into focus several key ideas: that readers bring their own text to each story; that words matter, especially in building images and thus the reality of the text; and that verisimilitude exists only as long as both writer and reader are willing. Time and again, the *reality* of Olson's work in particular is suspended when the text intentionally calls attention to itself.

There are many fine and fanciful poems in *The Night I Dropped Shakespeare on the Cat*, including several of my favorites—"A Bee Is a Predicate with Wings," "Unconscious," "The Fabric of Fabrication," "Open House," and "Laundry." Olson's end-piece, "This Other World: An Essay on Artistic Autonomy" is in essence the *ars poetica* of the volume and should not be missed. If you prefer, it is a way into the volume, should you decide to read against the grain and read it first. "The poem exalts disobedience" after all.

—Rebecca Spears

Eduardo & "I"

Peter Johnson. Buffalo, NY: White Pine Press, 2006.
ISBN: 1-893996-46-8

Peter Johnson, past editor of *The Prose Poem,* is one of the most influential and important voices working (as editor, theoretician, and practitioner) in the genre, and his most recent book, *Eduardo & "I,"* is his most ambitious and accomplished to date. It is both playful and meditative, and (as we should expect from Johnson) it models a variety of ideas about the way prose poems work—and perhaps about ways in which they don't. I can't probe all of this in a brief review, but I can give some sense of what's at stake here by looking at one of Johnson's most prominent features—his attraction to the doppelganger, doubling, splitting, and mirroring. His use of such strategies is ubiquitous and complex, and seems to be working both at an intuitive level and an analytic level—levels of poetic process and of structural vision and revision. In other words, these strategies comprise a kind of master trope for deploying the full range of his thinking.

That much is clear in Johnson's Laughlin-Award-winning *Miracles & Mortifications.* Not only does the title itself indicate a split, but the book is divided into two sections titled "Travels with Gigi" and "Travels with Oedipus"—duos are thus all over the project. (And "Gigi" is herself a multiple, two gi's or g's [which may be related, whether intuitively or analytically, to Johnson's coinage, "the g-spot of the poem"]).

Both "Travels with Gigi" and "Travels with Oedipus" trace an out-and home-again narrative path, the first both beginning and ending its journey through the world's cities with poems called "Home," the other resolving its chronological sequence of poems keyed to historical figures with "Return." One section marking travels in space, the other travels through time, *Miracles & Mortifications* is a prose-poem reduction of two great prose odes to space and time, *Invisible Cities* and *Einstein's Dreams,* with a third eye canted in the direction of Lowell's *History.*

Eduardo & "I" is also made up of two (untitled) parts, the first of which consists of 24 numbered poems written in the first person singular and featuring a (mostly?) imaginary friend named Eduardo who does service as the speaker's irresponsible, shape-shifting, loose-living alter ego. Sometimes he's referred to as Eddie, and some of these times he appears to be a dog.

If that description sounds a bit like John Berryman's description of his own alter ego, Henry, in the preface to his *Dream Songs,* it should. Johnson draws on the resources of the sixties/seventies "polyvoiced poem" (it's W. D. Snodgrass's term) in which the writerly self gets split or fragmented into a complex and ambiguous multiplicity of voices whose interaction dramatizes (as it lyricizes) the psychological, professional, and social crises of the poems' "author." These poems in part I are often jumpy and wildly playful in their verbal patterning, exploiting Johnson's gifts for punning gamesmanship, eccentric shifts of attention and voice, and manic allusiveness. That, too, could describe *The Dream Songs,* but *Eduardo & "I"* feels much less terror-driven and (frankly) mad than Berryman's work. Johnson also alludes to the Borges of "Borges and I," a very different, much soberer (both figuratively and literally) character than Berryman's personae, but part I of *Eduardo & "I"* doesn't feel like Borges's spooky double, either. Johnson's masks seem more a self-conscious effort to liberate the "I" from its own entrenchments and anxieties through rapidfire association and wordplay. But these very tactics, which make the poems funny and engaging, detach them from anything like a coherent logic or politics—this is not a criticism, but a recognition of what feels like an accomplished sense of purpose: play as escape from or alternative to reality.

But as Johnson has pointed out in interviews, these poems were written just prior to and in the year following 9/11, and the book projects a profound discomfort with the ludic disseminations of part I. Part II, in fact, at first seems wrenchingly inappropriate, a bizarre mismatch to the tone and spirit of part I (he closes part I with an allusion to Frankenstein's monster, an indication, I think, that he is quite aware of the grotesque structure he has chosen). Like *Miracles & Mortifications,* with comic Gigi (the space girl) contrasted with tragic Oedipus (the king of time), *Eduardo & "I"* is addressing serious questions in two very different ways. Here Johnson's theoretical sophistication is most evident, for the two parts actually dispose two distinct genres—the polyvoiced poem and the meditative (Wordsworthian) lyric—in a face-off that is also a collaboration. This begins with the titles of the books, both propounding two terms, in tension, separated and bound together. It reaches even to their matching ampersands, both of which do double duty—standing guard between the crucial terms they bind together, throwing ironized symbols back and forth over their formal barriers. They speak, in other words, about the ways in which form and thematic substance address each other in poems—a critical question for any serious writer.

So what does Johnson come up with in this recurring standoff between polyglossic disengagement and meditative engagement? Is part II a repudiation of part I, or a counterpart, or mirror image, or (more or less faint) echo? The answer to this may also lie in the title, or our interpretation of it. For its most obvious provocation is those quotes around the I. Their significance, I think, is also obvious: the "I" is a persona like any other, just another mask. And in this way of thinking, the title of the book basically refers to the crisis of subjectivity worked through (but not out) in part I.

But the polyvoiced poem always addresses subjectivity through its network of personae. We tend to assume that the Eduardo-personae and the "I"-persona are related in ways that constitute or define the psychological backdrop of whatever else is going on in the poems, and that these in turn speak in some way to an "author," with "intentions." The personae (all of them, the "I" included) polyangulate all substantial questions raised by the poem, bouncing and trapping every utterance in a complex of ironies, dramatizations, constructions and deconstructions. So in order to fathom Johnson's "I," we need to ask, "what kind of construction is Eduardo?" The answer part I gives is "multifarious and o.k." This will feel to some like a cheat, because to the extent that Eduardo's complexity addresses an actual world, it is as a gamester, someone who prefers not to pay attention, who has better things, funkier things, on his mind. These skittish poems use their multiplicity of masks and voices to erect a scaffolding of play over grim facticity. The tone shifts so often, so suddenly, and so ludically that the section seems a kind of paean to itself, to the grasshopper's strategy of singing one's way through the darkness.

Thus the second half of the book, which is much more meditative, with a tone of self-reflexive (and sometimes self-directed) anger and misery, felt like a let-down after the obsessive play of part I. After the flyaway pleasures of part I, part II seems sunk in despair and trapped in its own frame.

But the third poem in part II, "The Half-Full, Half-Empty Episode," provides a hint that changes the stakes wagered between the two halves. The poem's title of course alludes to that great question of attitude and perception, "do you see the glass as half-empty or half-full?" The poem, meanwhile, perhaps responding to its counterpart in part I, no. III, with its refrain of "you can't get theah from heah," is built around an odd repeating figure: "Hello from the City where. . . ." The poem ignores its own title except for this: "'The correct answer,' my wife explains, 'is that the glass contains water.'" And then it closes, "Hello from the City where certainty can be found in a rose, in the burnt portion of a cheese omelet, in the matching yellow headbands of two long-stemmed roses, in a lousy glass of water." Johnson has in fact raised this same question explicitly in his interview with Stephen Frech in *Another Chicago Magazine.* Concerning his earlier book, *Pretty Happy!,* Johnson says:

> According to the New Agers, the answer to the question of

whether the glass is half-filled or half-empty is that there is water in the glass. That's a nice philosophy to live by, but it makes for lousy literature. I'm after a dark irony related to the absurd. I try to avoid that fashionable cynicism or superficial cleverness we see everywhere in our culture.

In other words, part II contrasts part I's directionless world entirely expressed through masks, poses, and insubstantial voices with a world of distinct Cities in which an angry, focused eye searches for "certainty," but doesn't pretend to achieve it. Johnson can't commit to either mode—the polyvoiced poem or the Wordsworthian meditation—and opts, instead, to frame them as separate 24-poem sequences that mirror, speak to, and critique each other. In this model, the "I" of the book's title refers both to its behavior in the first section and to its efforts at mastery in part II. It is not simply one function in a polyvoiced complex focused on "Eduardo," but also a distinct problem in itself, the "I" of the subjective lyric, stumbling on itself, mirroring itself, betraying itself, and above all keeping itself honest.

—*Jerry McGuire*

A Fluxifyin' Concoction, PP/FF: can we have our say and play it too?

Peter Conners. *PP/FF: An Anthology.* Buffalo NY: Starcherone Books, 2006.

"Even if I was lucky enough to concoct an original thought, where would I put it?" asks Thom Ward's playful piece, "The Invention of Where," in the anthology *PP/FF.* We know that originality and innovation are privileged in western culture. And humans do tend to "put," to name, map, define and categorize things (though it is not certain exactly why: it may be because we are socialized to it, learning it in our schooling, so to maintain a tradition and systematizing method; or it may be that, like other predators, we survive better by categorizing, by systematizing what crosses our horizons—thus we need to recognize and deal with that tendency when it grows out of hand). But where and how do we make something original in our existence, our pre-defined, boundaried and categorized episteme?

There are interesting ironies packed into Ward's question, given that "thought" is a function of language/image, and language is originally acquired only from subjective exposure and immersion in it. So, as the question's irony indicates, concocting an "original thought" seems unlikely, at best—seemingly a matter of luck more than of cognitive endeavor—and, at worst, qualified by an "even if": a lead-in for the self's or others' persuasive pet illusions. So much for western culture's emphasis on originality and innovation—these may only be illusive. But not so fast: Ward's question comes at the end of a series of other questions highlighting paradoxes both mundane and transcendental, conveyed in prose poetry. So, prose poetry as exploratory form would seem to be not only the vehicle for this ambiguous, ironic (yet not), question but also one of its answers, in that an answer is a destination, a topoi, a "where." Fair enough. Yet shouldn't we be asking, as *PP/FF*'s editor Peter Connors does, what kind of "where" does prose poetry evoke and enact? Who decides the "where" of any piece of writing?—its (here, experimenting) writer, or the tendentious cultural authority of the academic interpretative system?

According to Connors, prose poetry and its inter-animating counterpart, flash fiction, have suffered a hobbling disservice in being confined, via the historical conventions of academe, by classification into genres. The two forms of writing are known for "where" they are defined and located ("pinned and wriggling"!) on the categorical map that primarily serves academic literary analysis, rather than being appreciated for their changeable, self-defining performativity. As such, they are voracious romps: actions—lively, ongoing, rhetorical interactions deeply motivated by the drives and affects of a universal human psyche where, for example, Orphism drives poetic endeavor. Prose poetry, I take Connors as saying, should be understood less as a particular categorical thing with defining characteristics that make it distinct from other particular things, but mostly for its performative actions in field of lively differences among semiotic relations. Experimental writing, it follows, should be understood for *what it does* in attempting to operate freely as an originating, artful, intentional form of "flux." Confinement to an academic definition, Connors insists, carries a lot of "old baggage" from western tradition, making the prose poem seem static and leaving little room for writerly innovation, little room for the "expanding of the parameters of what constitutes a prose poem or a flash fiction." This semiotic flux is buoyant, necessitates expansion. It thrives on uncertainty rather than on the certainty of a grounded definition: it is like being "balanced on a teeter-totter that never lands." Thus, each work in the carefully made selection of *PP/FF* offers, as it were, a new turn on the teeter-totter, a newly voracious romp through a semiotic flux that breeds hybrids of prose poetry, flash fiction, and countless new horizons on writerly play.

In the remarkably buoyant *PP/FF* much of the work tunes up and twangs with not only the surreal, but hybridization. The surreal observes itself, even parodying itself, for example, in relation to other forms such as narrative, or the ancient forms of storytelling, such as the moralizing fable. But those are mere genres. The work moves so quickly and admirably in and out of these topoi that categorization is not only impossible, but futile. Kenneth Bernard's "Sister Francetta and the Pig Baby," has a touch of this innovatively surreal tendency, a surrealism seemingly admiring itself, beaming in on its very own darling offspring:

> When Sister Francetta was a little girl she looked into a baby carriage one day and saw a baby with a pig head. . . . Now Sister Francetta taught us her morality through stories. . . . Strange mutilations from strange accidents were common. Sinful thoughts were the hardest to protect against. . . . The pig baby is still with me. It was different from her other stories. For example, it had no moral. It was just there: there had once been a baby with a pig head. . . . [W]hat I know can be listed very quickly:
>
> The pig baby was apparently Caucasian.
>
> Its parents were proud of it and in public seemed totally unaware of its pig head.
>
> I do not know how long it lived. It apparently never went to school.
>
> It always snorted noticeably but never let out any really pig-like sounds like *oink*.
>
> It ate and drank everything a regular baby ate and drank.
>
> Its parents were not Catholic.
>
> Everyone pretended not to notice that the baby had a pig

head. For some reason it was not talked about either.

At some early point the family either moved away or disappeared.

No one said anything about that either.

Surrealism was made to be irreverent about many things, but also about surrealism, wasn't it? In so doing, Bernard's flash fiction seems to be asking, can it co-exist on a teeter-totter with others such as the ancient art of fabulism? In the meantime, can the result still skewer the subtle or mostly overlooked yet nonetheless cruel, simpleminded moralistic forms of othering?   The works of Ward and Bernard are only two examples of innovative work in *PP/FF*, which overflows with similarly exceptional work that questions and then questions the questioner. It is a beautifully complicated anthology of *fluxifyin'* work. It shows that as writers we *can* have our say and play it, too. One of the strongest things a written work of art can do is to make its readers want to write in turn. This volume makes me want to write with innovation. Not only that. It also makes me want to say, hey: pass that can of spray paint, make it the red one – I know a few walls that could use some *fluxifyin'*.

—*Chris Murray*

Also Received

Prose. Formes poetiques contemporaines, #4. Les Impressions Nouvelles, Paris and Brussels. June 2006.

Alexander, Robert. *What the Raven Said.* Buffalo: White Pine Press, 2006.

Bogel, Ann and mIEKAL aND. *XAM.* West Lima, WI: Xexoxial Editions, 2005.

Doppelt, Suzanne. *Ring Rang Wrong.* tr. Cole Swenson. Burning Deck: Providence: 2006.

Lubasch, Lisa. *Twenty-One After Days.* Penngrove, CA: Avec Books, 2006.

Bouvier, Geoff. *Living Room.* Philadelphia: *American Poetry Review,* 2005.

Loydell, Rupert. *Ex Catalogue.* Lancaster, UK: Shadowtrain Books, 2006.
—*A Fire in the House of Ice.* NP: Snowblind Books, 2006.

Wiloch, Thomas. *Screaming in Code.* Pawleys Island, SC: Naked Snake Press, 2006.
—*Stigmata Junction.* Pawleys Island, SC: Naked Snake Press, 2006.

Gholson, Christien. *On the Side of the Crow.* New York: Hanging Loose Press, 2006.

Markus, Peter. *Good Brother.* New York: Calamari Press, 2006.

Potvin, P. F. *The Attention Lessons.* No Tell Books: NP, 2006.

Robinson, Elizabeth. *Under that Silky Roof.* Burning Deck: Providence, 2006.

White, Derek. *Poste Restante.* New York: Calamari Press, 2006.

Ratner, Rochelle. *Balancing Acts.* East Rockaway, NY: Marsh Hawk Press, 2006.

Damon, Maria and mIEKAL aND. *Literature Nation.* Bedford, MA: Potes & Poets Press, 2003.

_____

Send review copies of titles published during or after 2005 (two copies of each title, if possible) to *Sentence*, c/o Firewheel Editions, Box 7, Western Connecticut State University, 181 White St., Danbury, CT 06810.

Bibliography

Articles in Print and Online Journals

Acquisto, Joseph. "'Sowing some roses on the thorns of life:' Desire, Nature, Interpretation, and Judgement in Sade and Baudelaire." *Romance Studies*, Mar2006, Vol. 24 Issue 1: 15-27.

Bonnefoy, Yves. "Beyond words." *Times Literary Supplement*, 8/12/2005 Issue 5341: 13.

Dyer, Jeffrey. "Bad Dreams: Pushing Nothingness to Nobody." *Double Room* 7. http://www.webdelsol.com/DoubleRoom/7/Bad_Dreams.pdf, 2007.

Esdale, Logan. "Gertrude Stein, Laura Riding and the Space of Letters." *Journal of Modern Literature*, Summer2006, Vol. 29 Issue 4: 99-123.

Frémy, Yann. "Vers l'enfer (sur les proses dites 'évangéliques')." *Studi Francesi*, 2005 May-Aug; 49 (2 [146]): 272-91.

Holmes, Anne. "Aux origines du poème en prose français: 1750-1850." *French Studies*, Apr2005, Vol. 59 Issue 2: 249-250.

Marmarelli, Trina. "Other Voices: Strategies of Spatial, Temporal, and Psychological Distancing in the Early French Prose Poem." *Pacific Coast Philology*, 2005; 40: 57-76.

Moore, Fabienne. "Baudelaire et les poemes en prose du dix-huitièmè siècle: De Fénelon à Chateaubriand. *Bulletin Baudelairien on Prose Poetry,* 2005 Apr-Dec; 40 (1-2): 113-43.

Santilli, N. "The Prose Poem in Great Britain." *Poetry International Web*, http:uk.poetryinternationalweb.org, November 2006.

Scappettone, Jennifer. "Site Surfeit: Office for Soft Architecture Makes the City Confess." *Chicago Review*, Spring 2006, Vol. 51/52 Issue 4/1: 70-76.

Tursi, Mark. "New Brutalism's 'Smoke and Mirror': the Saga and Failure of potential Literary (non) Movement. *Double Room* 7. http://www. webdelsol.com/DoubleRoom/7/Bad_Dreams.pdf, 2007.

Articles in Books

Cepedello Moreno, Ma Paz. "Ocnos: Un diario poético." *Nostalgia de una patria imposible: Estudios sobre la obra de Luis Cernuda.* Ed. Juan Matas Caballero, José Enrique Martínez Fernández, José Manuel Trabado, Natalia Alvarez Méndez, Pablo Carriedo Castro. Madrid, Spain: Akal, 2005. 221-32.

Vincent-Munnia, Nathalie. "La Bohémienne, figure poétique en prose (Chez Aloysius Bertrand, Charles Baudelaire et les autres poètes en prose du XIXe siècle)." *La Bohémienne, figure poétique de l'errance aux XVIIIe et XIXe siècles*. Ed. Pascale Auraix-Jonchière and Gérard Loubinoux. Clermont-Ferrand, France: PU Blaise Pascal, 2005. 389-400.

Readers are invited to submit bibliographical citations to be listed in future issues of *Sentence*. Please limit citations to material published no earlier than June 2005.

Contributor Notes

Abe Hinako was born in Tokyo and began writing poetry in 1983. She has published three volumes of poetry, including *Umiyoubi no onna-tachi* (*Women on Seaday*) (2001), which won the coveted Takami Jun Prize.

Joe Ahearn is the author of *Five Fictions* (Sulphur River Review Press) and *sin-thet-ik* (Firewheel Editions Press). He is a James A. Michener Fellow in Poetry at the University of Texas at Austin.

Kazim Ali is the author of a book of poetry, *The Far Mosque,* winner of Alice James Books' New England/New York Award, and a novel, *Quinn's Passage,* named one of The Best Books of 2005 by *Chronogram* magazine. His poetry and essays have appeared in many journals, including *Colorado Review, The Iowa Review,* and *New Orleans Review.* He is the co-founder and publisher of the small press Nightboat Books and is currently assistant professor of English and Creative Writing at Shippensburg University of Pennsylvania.

Jeffrey Angles is head of the Japanese language program at Western Michigan University and co-editor of *Japan: A Traveler's Literary Companion* (Whereabouts Press, 2006). His *From a Woman of a Distant Land: Poetry and Prose of Tada Chimako* is forthcoming from Green Integer.

Erica Anzalone is a graduate of the Iowa Writers' Workshop. She currently teaches at Drake University. Her poems have appeared in *Denver Quarterly, Pleiades, Konundrum Engine Literary Review,* and elsewhere.

Sally Ashton is editor of the *DMQ Review,* an online journal that features poetry and art (www.dmqreview.com). Recent poetry and reviews have appeared in *Mississippi Review, Dos Passos Review, failbetter. com* and *Another Chicago Magazine,* as well as her chapbook, *These Metallic Days* from Mainstreet Rag.

Edward Bartók-Baratta's work has appeared in *African American Review, Denver Quarterly, Jacket, Ploughshares,* and elsewhere. He lives in Massachusetts.

Bill Berkson's recent books include *Gloria,* with etchings by Alex Katz (Arion Press, 2005); *The Sweet Singer of Modernism & Other Art Writings* (Qua Books, 2004); and an epistolary collaboration with Bernadette Mayer, *What's Your Idea of a Good Time?: Letters & Interviews 1977-1985* (Tuumba, 2006). Also just out are a collection of new poems *Our Friends Will Pass Among You Silently* (The Owl Press) and *Sudden Address: Selected Lectures* (Cuneiform Press). Berkson is a corresponding editor for Art in America and was Distinguished Paul Mellon Lecturer for 2006 at the Skowhegan School of Painting and Sculpture. He lives in New York and San Francisco and has taught at the San Francisco Art Institute since 1984.

Raymond L. Bianchi is a native of Chicago, the child of immigrants from Italy. His poems have appeared in *26, Another Chicago Magazine, Birddog, Antennae, The Economist, Moria* and many other journals. In 2007 Ray's collection of Brazilian Poetry in translation appeared as a featured section in *Aufgabe* magazine. He is the author of *Circular Descent* (Blaze Vox Press, 2004) and the chapbook *American Master* (Moria Books, 2006). Ray is the publisher of Cracked Slab Books of Chicago and Editor of Chicagopostmodernpoetry.com; he lives in Oak Park, IL.

Daniel Borzutzky is the author of *The Ecstasy of Capitulation* (BlazeVox Books, 2007) and *Arbitrary Tales* (Triple Press, 2005); and he is the translator of *Port Trakl* (forthcoming, Action Books) by Chilean poet Jaime Luis Huenún. His translations of early twentieth century Chilean prose writer Juan Emar can be found in *Conjunctions, Fence, Words Without Borders, Denver Quarterly,* and elsewhere. He lives in Chicago.

Geoff Bouvier's first book, *Living Room,* was selected by Heather McHugh as the winner of the 2005 APR/Honickman Prize. His writings have appeared in *American Poetry Review, Barrow Street, Denver Quarterly, jubilat, New American Writing, Western Humanities Review,* and *VOLT.* He received an MFA from Bard College's Milton Avery Graduate School of the Arts in 1997. He lives in San Diego, where he waits tables at Tapenade Restaurant and publishes journalistic prose for *The San Diego Reader.*

Brian Brennan lives and works in Norfolk, Virginia. His poems, stories, and reviews have appeared in this and other journals. He is at work on a novel.

Steve Bradbury's third book of translations, *Feelings Above Sea Level: Prose Poems from the Chinese of Shang Qin*, was recently published by Zephyr Press. He teaches at National Central University in Taiwan.

Jenny Browne is a James Michener Fellow in poetry at the University of Texas in Austin. Her most recent collection, *The Second Reason*, is forthcoming from the University of Tampa in 2007. She has recent poems in *Court Green, The Florida Review,* and *Poet Lore.*

Christopher Buckley's 15th book, *Modern History: Prose Poems 1987-2007,* will be published in 2008 by Tupelo Press. With Alexander Long, he edited *A Condition of the Spirit the Life and Work of Larry Lewis* (Eastern Washington University Press, 2004). He teaches in the creative writing program at the University of California, Riverside.

Kevin Cantwell teaches poetry and book history at Macon State College in Georgia. His poems have appeared in *The New Republic, Paris Review, 32 Poems, Ninth Letter, Commonweal,* and many other places. His book, *Something Black in the Green Part of Your Eye,* was published by New Issues in 2002.

Ch'oe Sŭng-ja is one of South Korea's most prominent writers and the first woman poet to be published in *Munhak kwa jisŏng,* a leading journal of dissent during the 70s-80s.

Don Mee Choi's *When the Plug Gets Unplugged,* a chapbook of Kim Hyesoon's poetry in English translation, is available from Tinfish Press. Her *Anxiety of Words: Contemporary Poetry by Korean Women* was recently published by Zephyr Press. She lives in Seattle.

Peter Conners' (www.peterconners.com) prose poetry collection *Of Whiskey and Winter* is forthcoming from White Pine Press. He edited *PP/FF: An Anthology* (Starcherone Books, 2006) and is founding co-editor of the literary journal, *Double Room.* He lives in Rochester, NY where he works at BOA Editions.

Alexander Cuadros is a writer and translator living in New York City. His translation of an excerpt from Argentinian writer Tununa Mercado's *La Madriguera* is forthcoming in *Review: Literature and Arts of the Americas.*

Mark Cunningham lives near Charlottesville, VA. His poems have recently appeared in *Alice Blue* and *Dusie.* He has published two chapbooks, one on the Mudlark website and one titled *Second Story,* on the Right Hand Pointing website. Forthcoming from Tarpaulin Sky Press is his book tentatively titled *Body Language,* containing two separate collections, one titled "Body," (on parts of the body) and one titled "Primer," (on numbers and letters).

Chloë Daimyo is an Alumni Member at the University of Oregon, having served as a Professional Cultural Researcher and academic diplomat (2002-2007). Her work has taken in such topics as the disappearing girls of Gion, Kyoto, Japan.

Jon Davis has published five collections of poetry, including *Scrimmage of Appetite,* for which he was awarded a 1998 Lannan Literay Award in Poetry. He recently completed three new manuscripts, *The Immortals, Hetronymy: An Anthology,* and *Autohagiography: The Poems of Chuck Calabreze.* Poems have appeared in recent issues of *Chokecherries, Dragonfire, Indiana Review* (under heteronym Chuck Calabreze's byline), *Ontario Review, American Letters & Commentary* (under heteronym Felicia DuBois' byline), and *The New Hampshire Review.*

Neil de la Flor's work has appeared recently or is forthcoming in the *Indiana Review, Hotel Amerika, Court Green, Hayden's Ferry Review,* and *Threecandles.com.* Neil is the co-author of *Facial Geometry* (NeO Pepper Press), a chapbook of collaborate triads written with Maureen Seaton and Kristine Snodgrass. He lives in Miami, FL and is a fashion designer by day.

Carrie Etter is an Associate Lecturer in Creative Writing at Bath Spa University, where she has introduced an undergraduate course on the prose poem and short-short story, "Sudden Prose." She has recently completed work on *Imagined Sons,* consisting primarily of prose poems, and has prose poems published or forthcoming in *All That Mighty Heart: London Poems* (University of Virginia, 2008), *Aufgabe, Barrow Street, The Liberal, PN Review, Poetry Review,* and elsewhere.

A Professor of English at CUNY-LaGuardia, Thomas Fink is the author of two books of criticism, most recently *A Different Sense of Power* (Fairleigh Dickinson UP, 2001) and four books of poetry, including *No*

Appointment Necessary (Moria Poetry, 2006). In the Fall, Fairleigh Dickinson University Press will publish a collection of essays on David Shapiro's work that he and Joseph Lease edited. Fink's paintings hang in various collections.

Kass Fleisher is the author of *The Bear River Massacre and the Making of History* (nonfiction; SUNY Press, 2004); *Accidental Species: A Reproduction* (conceptual memoir; Chax Press, 2005); *The Adventurous* (conceptual memoir; Factory School, 2007); and *Talking Out of School: Memoir of an Educated Woman* (forthcoming from Dalkey Archive Press in 2008).

Charles Fort holds the Distinguished Paul W. Reynolds and Clarice Kingston Reynolds Endowed Chair in Poetry and is Professor of English at the University of Nebraska at Kearney. Anthologies and awards include: *The Best American Poetry 2003, The Best American Poetry 2000, The Best of the Prose Poem: An International Journal 2000, MacDowell Fellow 1996, Poetry Society of America, Poetry Award 1990,* the *Randall Jarrell Poetry Prize 1985,* and twenty-five other anthologies. He has published twelve books of poetry, including *Frankenstein Was A Negro, Prose Poems* (Loganhouse Press 2002), and *The Town Clock Burning,* which was reprinted by Carnegie Mellon University Press in the Classic Contemporary Series, 1991.

Angela Jane Fountas writes, teaches, and runs Write-Habit.org. She is also a volunteer at 826 Seattle. Her work has appeared or is forthcoming in *Red Mountain Review, elimae, The Bitter Oleander, Diagram, Pindeldyboz, Redivider,* and elsewhere. She recently received grants from 4Culture and the Office of Arts and Cultural Affairs in Seattle and holds an MFA in creative writing from the University of Alabama.

James Fowler, with the reluctant acceptance of his wife, does nothing but write, teach, and occasionally edit poetry. She works and he is a retired Navy senior-chief, so they do not starve. They live in Charlestown, N.H. His poems have appeared widely, including *Worcester Review, Paragraph,* and *Contemporary Haibun.* Jim has won a Poetry Society of New Hampshire National Poetry Contest.

Alex Galper was born in Kiev, Ukraine and came to America at the age of 19. He had to keep on playing with words in the only language that he knew—Rus-

sian, and hope that one day it would be recognized in his homeland. After all, where else? In 1996, he graduated from Brooklyn College majoring in Creative Writing (his professor was Allen Ginsberg). English translations of his texts have appeared in over 30 magazines in the USA and UK, whereas in Russia, he is considered too marginal, extreme, and "too-American" to publish. Go figure... He hopes that nothing got lost in translation.

Christine Gelineau is the author of *Remorseless Loyalty (2006)*, winner of the Richard Snyder Prize. She co-edited *French Connections: A Gathering of Franco-American Poets* (forthcoming in 2007). Her poetry, essays and reviews have appeared widely. Gelineau teaches at Binghamton University and in the low-residency graduate writing program at Wilkes University.

Daniel Grandbois was born in Minnesota and raised in Colorado, where he lives today. *The Hermaphrodite (An Hallucinated Memoir)*, with forty original woodcuts by renowned Argentine printmaker Alfredo Benavidez Bedoya and translated into Spanish by Liliana Valenzuela, is forthcoming from Green Integer in September 2007. *Unlucky Lucky Days*, a collection of prose poems and absurd tales, is forthcoming from BOA Editions in October 2008. Also a musician, Daniel has played upright bass for Tarantella, a middle-eastern/spaghetti-western band, and *Slim Cessna's Auto Club*, a yodeling punk/country band. Both are on Jello Biafra's Alternative Tentacles label.

James Grinwis has work in recent issues of *Quick Fiction, Turnrow, New Orleans Review, Double Room, Greensboro Review, Columbia,* and elsewhere. He is founding editor of *Bateau*, a new journal.

Kelle Groom's poetry collections are *Underwater City* (University Press of Florida, 2004) and *Luckily* (Anhinga Press, 2006). Her poems have appeared in *Court Green, DoubleTake, The New Yorker, Ploughshares, Poetry,* and *Witness.* She is grants administrator and communications coordinator for Atlantic Center for the Arts in New Smyrna Beach, Florida

Maurice Kilwein Guevara was born in Belencito, Colombia and raised in Pittsburgh, Pennsylvania. He teaches in the doctoral creative writing program at the University of Wisconsin—Milwaukee. His most recent collection is *Autobiography of So-*

and-so: Poems in Prose. "The Other Word for Thesaurus" comes from his current manuscript-in-progress, entitled *POEMA*.

Richard Gwyn was born in Wales. Poet, novelist and translator, he divides his time between his country of birth and Spain. His website can be found at www.richardgwyn.com.

Tanesia Hale-Jones is a graduate of the San Francisco State University MFA program, and her work has appeared in *Callaloo, Transfer,* and elsewhere. She lives in Oakland.

Kalev Hantsoo is a student at the University of Maryland, currently considering a focus in anthropology. This is his first publication.

Kevin Haworth's first novel, *The Discontinuity of Small Things,* was awarded the Samuel Goldberg Prize for best work of Jewish fiction by a writer under 40. He lives in Athens, Ohio with his wife and two children and teaches at Ohio University.

He Chuanfu's biographical details are kept under tight wraps, but the Chinese poet has ventured to say that his or her writing is "dedicated to all the lonely children."

Hirata Toshiko is one of Japan's most prominent feminist writers and the author of over ten books of poetry, fiction, essays, and award-winning plays. Her poetry has been translated into Chinese, English, Italian, Korean, and Russian.

Karen Holman works as a therapist at a community mental health center for people who have serious mental illness. Her hobbies are ice sculpture, astronomy, and heirloom gardening. She lives with her husband and two cats and can't get over the dwindling populations of honey bees, frogs, and fireflies.

Brooke Horvath teaches at Kent State University. *Lecture on Dust,* his third collection of poetry, has just been released by Bottom Dog Press.

Ann Howells is a board member of Dallas Poets Community, currently serving as secretary. She has been managing editor of its poetry journal, *Illya's Honey,* since 1999. In 2001, she was named a "Distinguished Poet of Dallas" by the Dallas Public Library. Her work has appeared in *Borderlands, Sulphur River Literary Review, Gertrude, Concho River, Mind Purge,*

Red River Review, and others.

Hsia Yü (sometimes spelled Xia Yu) lives in Taipei, where she makes her living as a song lyricist and translator. A bilingual volume of her verse, translated by Steve Bradbury, was published by Zephyr Press in 2001 under the title, *Fusion Kitsch: Poems from the Chinese of Hsia Yü.*

Hung Hung is a poet, translator, and director of many plays, operas, and award-winning films. He lives in Taipei, where he co-edits *Xianzai Shi (Poetry Now)* and curates the Taipei International Poetry Festival.

Itō Hiromi is a leading voice among Japan's younger, liberated women poets. She has published numerous volumes of poetry and prose, including two novellas that were short-listed for Japan's highest award for literary fiction. She now lives near San Diego.

David James teaches English at Oakland Community College in Michigan. His newest chapbook, *I Dance Back,* was published by March Street Press in 2002.

Jiao Tong is the author of half a dozen volumes of verse. He is Associate Professor of Chinese Literature at National Central University in Taiwan and founding editor of the culinary journal *Yinshi (Food and Drink).*

Brian Johnson is the author of *Self-Portrait.* He is the recipient of a Connecticut Commission on the Arts Fellowship. In addition to serving for several years as assistant editor of *The Prose Poem: An International Journal,* he has taught creative writing at Yale, Brown, Providence College, and Southern Connecticut State University, where he is currently assistant professor of English.

George Kalamaras is the author of six books of poetry and prose poetry, including *Even the Java Sparrows Call Your Hair* (Quale Press, 2004) and *Gold Carp Jack Fruit Mirrors* (The Bitter Oleander Press, forthcoming, 2008). He is the recipient of fellowships from the National Endowment for the Arts (1993) and the Indiana Arts Commission (2001). He is Professor of English at Indiana University-Purdue University Fort Wayne, where he has taught since 1990.

Kasuya Eiichi is Japan's foremost proponent of the prose poem and one of the few poets to write exclusively in this genre. His collection *Sekai no kōzō* (*The Structure of the World*) (1971) is a contemporary classic.

Luke Kennard is a poet and an assistant lecturer at the University of Exeter, England. His first book, *The Solex Brothers*, was published by Stride in 2005 and is out of print. His new collection, *The Harbour Beyond the Movie*, is out now from Salt Books. He won an Eric Gregory award in 2005.

Jill Khoury has lived in Pittsburgh and studied at Ohio State. Her work has appeared in the *Flat City Anthology*, nidus, and elsewhere.

Kim Hyesoon is Korea's foremost feminist poet and the first woman poet to receive the Kim Su-yŏng Poetry award, South Korea's highest literary honor. She teaches creative writing at Seoul College of the Arts.

Rauan Klassnik was born driving through evergreen. It snows inside his brain every day. The sun, he's told, will come again. His poems have appeared or are forthcoming in *MiPoesias, Sleeping-Fish, Pilot Poetry, The Mississippi Review, The Santa Clara Review, No Tell Motel*, and others.

Michael Koshkin lives in Boulder with Jennifer Rogers, where they run Hot Whiskey Press. In 2006, he published the chapbooks *Parad e R ain* (Big Game Books) and *The Subtraction of Light (for a pig)* (Wyrd Tree Press). He has also worked on the editorial boards for *Bombay Gin* (the official Naropa magazine) and *Bimbo Gun* (the bastard Naropa magazine).

Richard Kostelanetz is an artist, musician, film-maker, and author of dozens of books. He has beena Guggenheim Fellow and a Fulbright Scholar, and he is a respected critic of avant-garde art and literature.

David Lazar's books include *The Body of Brooklyn, Conversations with M.F.K. Fisher,* and *Michael Powell: Interviews*. Forthcoming are an anthology, *Truth in Nonfiction* (Iowa), and a book of prose poems, *Powder Town* (Pecan Grove). His work has appeared in *Southwest Review, Denver Quarterly, Pleiades, Gulf Coast, Arts & Letters, Best of the Prose Poem* and other journals and magazines. He teaches

at Columbia College Chicago, and is the editor of *Hotel Amerika*.

Andrea Lingenfelter has translated several volumes of contemporary Chinese writing, including Mian Mian's "glamlit" novel *Candy* (Back Bay Books, 2003) and Lilian Lee's *Farewell My Concubine* (William Morrow, 1993). She lives in Seattle.

Liu Kexiang was born in Central Taiwan. Trained as a journalist, he worked for many years as an editor and is the author of numerous collections of verse, nature writing, and picture books, which he illustrates himself.

Robert Hill Long teaches at the Penn State University and is the author of *The Effigies* (prose poems from Plinth Books). His work has appeared in *The Best of the Prose Poem, New England Review, Kenyon Review, Zyzzyva,* and elsewhere.

Lu Xun (sometimes spelled Lu Hsün) was the most influential literary reformist in modern China and the author of the first book of original prose poetry written in Chinese. His fiction and satirical essays are famous for their biting wit. He died in 1936.

Mikhail Magazinnik is a poet/translator/performer. He is a member of the New York-based, vy da vy, artist collective. He came to the United States from the former USSR in 1989. His works have appeared in various UK, USA, Russian and Australian periodicals.

Jerry McGuire has published two books of poems, *The Flagpole Dance* (Lynx House) and *Vulgar Exhibitions* (Eastern Washington University). Much of his work is created and presented in collaboration with musicians, dancers, and visual artists. Most recently film-maker Allison Bohl and animator/painter Yeon Choi have produced works incorporating his poems, his voice, and his digital soundscapes. He teaches Creative Writing, poetics, and film studies at the University of Louisiana at Lafayette.

Sandy McIntosh's collections of poetry include *Forty-Nine Guaranteed Ways To Escape Death* (Sept. 2007), *The After-Death History of My Mother, Between Earth and Sky,* and several other books and chapbooks. His poetry and essays have been appeared in *The New York Times, Newsday, The Nation, the Wall Street Journal*, and elsewhere. His original poetry in a film script won the Silver Medal in the Film Festival of the Americas. He is Managing Editor of Marsh Hawk Press.

Michael Meyerhofer's first full-length manuscript, *Leaving Iowa*, won the Liam Rector First Book Award from Briery Creek Press. He is also the author of three chapbooks: *Cardboard Urn, The Right Madness of Beggars*, and *Real Courage*. He was recently the recipient of the James Wright Poetry Award, the Annie Finch Prize, and the Laureate Prize. His work has appeared in *Arts & Letters, Green Mountains Review, Fugue, North American Review, Asimov's Science Fiction Magazine*, and others.

Yuko Minamikawa Adams grew up in the Tokyo area and studied English at university. She has published two collections of poetry and writes both in Japanese and English. She now lives in Hertfordshire, England.

Chris Murray's writings can be found in *LIT, American Book Review, Sentence, Shampoo, Blaze Vox , Moria*, and many other magazines and journals. Chris publishes *Texfiles Press,* and with Hoa Nguyen & Susan Briante, Chris curates the print journal, *Super Flux*. Her 2007 book of poems is *Juffayr Avenue*, and a chapbook, *Meme Me Up, Scotty!*, appeared in 2004. For 4 years Chris has been the poet-blogger at *chris murray's Texfiles*. Chris is professor of English and coordinator of the College of Arts and Sciences for New York Institute of Technology, Bahrain Campus.

Steve Myers's poetry collection, *Memory's Dog*, appeared from FootHills Publishing in 2004; his chapbook, *Work Site*, was published by FootHills in 2003. Individual poems have recently appeared or will soon appear in *Atlanta Review, caesura, The Dark Horse, Ekphrasis, Kestrel*, and *The Southern Review*, as well as in the anthology *Common Wealth: Contemporary Poets on Pennsylvania*. His four-prose-poem sequence *Bloc* recently won the Robert J. DeMott Short Prose Prize sponsored by *Quarter After Eight*. He is Professor of English at DeSales University in Center Valley.

Sawako Nakayasu was born in Yokohama, Japan but has spent most of her life in the States. Her book-length poem *So We Have Been Given Time   Or* was the winner of the Verse Prize for 2003. She is editor-in-chief of the literary journal *Factorial*.

Andrew Neuendorf's work has appeared in *Double Room, Northwest Review, Measure, Effing Magazine, Kadar Koli*, and *McSweeney's Internet Tendency*. He lives in Austin, Texas.

Ed Orr's work has appeared recently in *Denver Quarterly* and *California Quarterly*. He says, "Aside from a compulsion to connect in the Aristotelian sense of metaphor, I am virtually without qualitities."

Virgilio Piñera (1912–1979) was a Cuban novelist, playwright, poet, short-story writer, and essayist who published over twenty-five books during his lifetime. Cofounder of the important Cuban literary magazine *Ciclón*, he is said to have greatly influenced the work of Reinaldo Arenas, author of *Before Night Falls*. In large part due to his open homosexuality, during the last nine years of Piñera's life his work was censored by the Cuban government, his name forbidden from being mentioned in conferences, essays, and classes.

Emma Ramey is an assistant poetry editor for *DIAGRAM* and lives in snow country. Her poems have recently appeared or will appear in *Typo, Rhino, Octopus*, and *The Mississippi Review*.

Jessy Randall is the Curator of Special Collections at Colorado College. Her poems have appeared in *Explosive Magazine, Mudfish*, and *Painted Bride Quarterly*. Her first full-length collection, *A Day in Boyland*, is now available from Ghost Road Press. She lives in Colorado Springs with her husband, two young children, and sister-in-law. personalwebs.coloradocollege.edu/~jrandall

Kristin Ryling is the author of "Trompe L'Oeil," (poems from Firewheel Editions), and a contributor to the first issue of *Sentence*. Other books include *Mnemes*, (The Complete Anthology), *1/2 0 = C, Scarlet Iodine*, and *Harlequins Pen for Dancinginstone*, all published through Lapin Press.

Catherine Sasanov is the author of *Traditions of Bread and Violence* (Four Way Books), *All the Blood Tethers* (Northeastern University Press), and the chapbook, *What's Left of Galgani* (Franciscan University Press). She was the librettist for *Las Horas de Belén: A Book of Hours*, commissioned by Mabou Mines. *Field, Salamander, Hotel Amerika, Quarter After Eight,* and *Skidrow Penthouse* all carried her work in 2006.

Igor Satanovsky is a bilingual Russian-American poet/translator/visual artist whose work appeared on both sides of the Atlantic. He edited 2 poetry books by Alex Galper for Koja Press, and authored his own volume of poetry in English, *American Poetry (free and how)*, Koja Press, 2002.

Hiroaki Sato was born in Japan but has lived in New York City since 1968. He is one of the most prolific translators of contemporary Japanese poetry, with dozens of volumes of translation to his name.

Liana Scalettar's fiction has appeared (or will appear shortly) in *American Short Fiction, Arts & Letters, drunkenboat.com, failbetter.com, gutcult.com, LIT,* and *Washington Square*. She teaches at Queens College and has also taught at Gotham Writers' Workshop and the Hudson Valley Writers' Center.

Siobhán Scarry's work has appeared in *jubilat, Greensboro Review, Mid-American Review,* and *Five Fingers Review,* among other journals. Poems are forthcoming in *P-Queue* and *Sentence* (#6). Her prose poems won Editors' Choice in *Mid-American Review*'s Fineline Competition in 2003, 2004, and 2005. She holds an MFA from the University of Montana and is currently pursuing a PhD in Literature at SUNY Buffalo, where she is finishing her first book of poetry and teaching as a poet-in-the-schools.

Matthew W. Schmeer edits *Poetry Midwest* and is an Assistant Professor of English at Johnson County Community College in Overland Park, Kansas.

James R. Scrimgeour is a Professor of English at Western Connecticut State University. He has published a critical biography of *Sean O'Casey* (G. K. Hall) and seven books of poetry. He served as Editor of Connecticut Review from September 1992 – September 1995. He resides in New Milford Connecticut with his wife, Christine Xanthakos Scrimgeour.

Shang Qin (sometimes spelled Shang Ch'in) was born in China in 1930 but has lived in Taiwan since the early fifties. His prose poems have been translated into English, Dutch, French, German, and Swedish.

Ravi Shankar is Poet-in-Residence at Central Connecticut State University and the founding editor of the international online journal of the arts, *Drunkenboat.com*. His first book of poems, *Instrumental-*

ity (Cherry Grove, 2004) was named a finalist for the 2005 Connecticut Book Awards. He has appeared as a commentator on NPR and Wesleyan Radio, published his critical and creative work in such places as the *Paris Review* and *Poets & Writers,* and along with Tina Chang and Nathalie Handal, is currently editing an anthology of contemporary Asian and Arab poetry, due out with W. W. Norton & Co. in 2007.

Jay Snodgrass lives in Tallahassee, FL with his wife and daughter. He is the author of two books of poetry, *Monster Zero* and *The Underflower*. In therapy for his fear of television sets and interstates, he is still pursued by Ghosts.

Rebecca Spears teaches creative writing with the University of Gävle (Sweden) and SMU's Continuing Education. Her writing has appeared in *Calyx, Minnesota Review, Natural Bridge, Nimrod, Borderlands, Texas Review,* and other journals.

D. E. Steward's "Novembir" is a month in a sequential project that runs month to month, underway since September 1986. This form is an attempt to note and build on some of the literary reality of the times. A hundred and fifty-five months are published in other literary magazines. A collection of short verse, *Torque,* appeared late last year from Kings Estate Press.

Julia Story's work has appeared in *The Iowa Review, Verse, Painted Bride Quarterly, Good Foot, Salt Hill,* and other publications. She lives in Bloomington, IN with her soon-to-be husband and their miniature dachshund.

Robert Strong works at a small technical college in a large state university system teaching communication skills to young Americans for our future. You can read his *Puritan Spectacle* (Elixir Press) for pleasure.

Wayne Sullins's poems and flash fiction have appeared in *Quick fiction, Poetry East, The Quarterly, Compost,* and many other journals. His book, *Najimi,* is available at www.wastelandpress.net. He has traveled widely, and now lives in Boston, raising a son, working on stories about Hanoi.

Suzuki Shirōyasu was born in Tokyo. He originally worked as a cameraman for the Japanese national broadcasting service but later became a professor of film-making at Tama Art University. He has published over twenty books of poetry.

Eileen R. Tabios has released over 20 volumes in various genres and media. Recipient of the Philippines' National Book Award for Poetry, she recently released *The Light Sang As It Left Your Eyes* (Marsh Hawk Press, 2007) and *SILENCES: The Autobiography of Loss* (Blue Lion, 2007). In her poetry, she has crafted a body of work that is unique for melding ekphrasis with transcolonialism. Her poems have been translated into Spanish, Tagalog, Japanese, Paintings, Video, Drawings, Visual Poetry, Mixed Media Collages, Kali Martial Arts, Modern Dance and Sculpture.

Takahashi Mutsuo came to international attention in the 1970s for his bold expressions of homoerotic desire. He is one of Japan's most thoroughly translated poets. His most recent book of English translations is *On Two Shores: New and Selected Poems* (Dedalus Press, 2006).

Tatehata Akira is a curator at the National Museum of Art in Osaka and one of the few Japanese poets to specialize in prose poetry. Hiroaki Sato translated a volume of Tatehata's prose poems under the title, *Runners in the Margins* (P.S., A Press, 2003).

Steve Timm has published chapbooks with Answer Tag Home Press, BlazeVOX, and Bronze Skull Press. He teaches English as a second language at the University of Wisconsin-Madison.

Nick Twemlow's poems have lately appeared or are forthcoming in *A Public Space, Boston Review, Fence,* and *Volt*. He is co-editor of *The Canary*, and recently spent a year in New Zealand as a Fulbright Fellow. He lives in Chicago, where he works as an editor.

Alexandra van de Kamp's work has appeared *Crab Orchard Review, Salt Hill, Washington Square,* and many other journals. Her chapbook, *The Rainiest May in the Twentieth Century*, was a winner of the 2001 Quentin R. Howard Poetry Prize from *Wind Magazine*. She is co-founding editor of *Terra Incognita*, a bilingual literary journal distributed in Spain and the United States. A new chapbook, *The Photographer's Interview*, was published by The Premier Poets Chapbook series in 2006. www.alexandra-vandekamp.com.

Monique van den Berg has taught poetry, literature, and writing at colleges in Wisconsin and California. She is currently a college instructor by day and an ad agency minion later in the day. While getting her MFA from New College of California, she co-edited the literary journal *Prosodia*. Her poems have appeared in numerous literary journals and are touring the country through 2008 as part of the Visual Verse project. She lives in Berkeley and writes online at mopie.com.

Xi Chuan is a widely published author of poems, essays, and translations. A major figure in mainland Chinese letters, he teaches literature at the Central Institute of Fine Arts in Beijing.

Mark Yakich is the author of *Unrelated Individuals Forming a Group Waiting to Cross,* (National Poetry Series, Penguin 2004) and *The Making of Collateral Beauty,* (Snowbound Chapbook Award, Tupelo 2006). markyakich.com.

Ye Mimi is a recent graduate of the National Dong Hwa University Graduate Institute of Creative Writing, which is the only creative writing program in Taiwan. Her first volume of poetry, *Qihei* (Pitch Dark), was published in 2004.

Yi Yŏn-ju is one of South Korea's most prominent feminist poets of the 1980s and early 1990s. She committed suicide in 1992.

Firewheel Editions Catalog

Mille et un sentiments by Denise Duhamel

perfect binding, 72 pages, ISBN 0-9665754-6-6, $12

Firewheel Editions is proud to present Denise Duhamel's new book, *Mille et un sentiments*.

"I feel that Denise Duhamel's poetry is a direct line to the laughing Dakinis in one of the heavenly realms (who cares which one); that her poetry is like main-lining some illicit drug, the kind you can never get enough of; that her poetry is a feast, a fiesta, a bliss-banque, fourth of July fireworks; that Denise's poetry is visionary, dazzling, a sensual-cerebral celebration. I feel as if I've been reinvented when I read Denise Duhamel, as if I can live on this planet when I read Denise Duhamel, as if I've met a kindred soul when I read Denise Duhamel. I feel the sharp edge of wit and honesty when I read Denise Duhamel. I feel that Denise's poetry will be outlawed, banned and burned by blue-blooded America!"

—Nin Andrews

The Book of Willie by Charles Kesler

perfect binding, 41 pages, ISBN 096657545-8, $10

Willie Williams is late-20th-century American culture boiled down to one hard-praying, hard-writing, hard-drinking Vietnam vet. Not necessarily in that order. This is his book, but don't tell his neighbors about it.

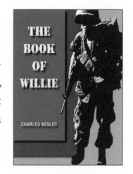

Best Texas Writing 1

perfect binding, 140 pages, ISBN 0-9656349-1-4, $10

A collection of the best poems, stories, and essays out of Texas. Includes work by Bruce Bond, Gerald Burns, Jack Myers, Naomi Shihab Nye, Kathleen Peirce, Pattiann Rogers, Frederick Turner, Marion Winik, and others. Edited by Joe Ahearn and Brian Clements. Rancho Loco Press.

Best Texas Writing 2

perfect binding, 221 pages, ISBN 0-9665754-1-5, $10

Second annual collection of the best poems, stories and essays from Texas. Includes work by Wendy Barker, Paul Christensen, Gillian Conoley, Dagoberto Gilb, Edward Hirsch, Judith Kroll, Walter McDonald, Robert Phillips, Matthew Sharpe, Laurel Speer, and others. Edited by Brian Clements.

The Future Called Something O'Clock by Daniel Luévano

saddlestitched, 26 pages, ISBN 0-9665754-0-7, $8

The poems in Daniel Luévano's premiere chapbook are "not so much a Gregorian chant or mambo / but diligence," a series of quiet explosions that shed light here and there toward "where I'm going when / I'm no longer like I am now." *Signed and numbered limited edition.*

Trompe L'Oeil by Kristin Ryling

loose in rice paper wrapper, 26 pages,
ISBN 0-9665754-2-3, $8

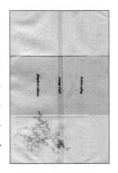

No one in the history of literature sounds like Kristin Ryling. These beautifully complex prose poems are collected like so many of the butterflies and moths whose names flitter through Ryling's poems on pristine pages in lovely rice paper wrapping. An unforgettable debut. *Signed and numbered, fine limited edition.*

Stitches by Rauan Klassnik

saddlestitched, 14 pages, ISBN 0-9665754-3-1, $8

Rauan Klassnik's poems dispense with ornament and drive straight down the emotional tracks, carrying along with them "stitched together in a sling" the fear and the hope that finding the perfect correlative in the world of objects "will carry you over the water."

sĭn·thĕt´·ĭk by Joe Ahearn

saddlestitched, 32 pages, ISBN 0-9665754-4-X, $10

Joe Ahearn's smart chapbook wrestles with the problem of what it means to be an alert and conscientious contemporary American poet. These poems, composed with "synthetic" methods, come from an American poet striving to discover the right path between the personal and the impersonal, between tradition and innovation. *Signed and numbered.*

sĭn · thĕt´ · ĭk

Joe Ahearn

Sentence: a Journal of Prose Poetics

perfect binding, ISSN 1545-5378, $12 one issue, $22 two issues, $30 three issues (subscriptions include shipping)

The premier magazine of the prose poem, dedicated to preserving and extending the traditions of the prose poem and "poet's prose."

Titles	Qty.	Cost

Subtotal $_____

Shipping $_____
($2 for first book, $0.75 for each additional book)

Total Amount Enclosed $_____

Name _____

Organization _____

Address _____

Phone _____

Email _____

Please send check or money order payable to:

Firewheel Editions
Box 7
Western Connecticut State University
181 White St.
Danbury, CT 06810

For more information, email **info@firewheel-editions.org**.
Books also available online at **www.firewheel-editions.org**.

Author Index

◯ Sentence 5